Values in Conflict
The University, the Marketplace, and the Trials of Liberal Education

Values in Conflict is a clarion call to policy makers, business leaders, and the public at large to rethink the current direction of the contemporary university. Paul Axelrod contends that liberal education, the core of higher learning, is threatened by the constricting pressures of the marketplace, and he explains how political and economic pressures are redefining higher learning.

Axelrod demonstrates how, in the race for riches – symbolized by endless rhetoric about the need for Canada to become globally competitive, technologically advanced, and proficient at churning out "knowledge workers" – our schools and universities are being forced by government policy to narrow their educational vistas. The decision-making autonomy that universities must have to provide cultural, intellectual, community-service, and training functions is being eroded. *Values in Conflict* explains why this is happening – and why it matters.

PAUL AXELROD is professor and dean of the Faculty of Education, York University. He is author of several books, including *The Promise of Schooling: Education in Canada, 1800–1914* and *Making a Middle Class: Student Life in English Canada during the Thirties.*

D1607650

Values in Conflict

The University, the Marketplace, and the Trials of Liberal Education

PAUL AXELROD

McGill-Queen's University Press
Montreal & Kingston • London • Ithaca

© McGill-Queen's University Press, 2002
ISBN 0-7735-2406-1 (cloth)
ISBN 0-7734-2407-X (paper)

Legal deposit first quarter 2002
Bibliothèque nationale du Québec

Printed in Canada on acid-free paper that is 100% ancient forest free (100% post-consumer recycled), processed chlorine free, and printed with vegetable-based, low VOC inks.

McGill-Queen's University Press acknowledges the support of the Canada Council for the Arts for its publishing program. It also acknowledges the financial support of the Government of Canada through the Book Publishing Industry Development Program (BPIDP).

National Library of Canada Cataloguing in Publication Data

Axelrod, Paul Douglas
    Values in conflict : the university, the marketplace and the trials
    of liberal education

Includes bibliographical references and index.
ISBN 0-7735-2406-1 (bound). – ISBN 0-7734-2407-X (pbk.)

    1. Education, Humanistic–Canada. 2. Education, Higher–Aims and
objectives–Canada. 3. Education, Higher–Economic aspects–Canada. I. Title.

LB2322.2.A94 2002   378'.012'0971   C2002-900124-2

This book was designed by David LeBlanc and typeset in 10/14 Sabon

This book is dedicated to my family whose love, support, humour, and wisdom sustain and uplift me: Susan, Kaitlyn, Morris, Ruthe, Sonny, Bess, Lynne, Jamie, Josh, Marla, Nick, Sandra, Rebecca, and Alex.

Contents

Tables

Acknowledgments

I have shown various versions of this manuscript to friends and colleagues who have, without fail, offered their comments, criticisms, suggestions, and encouragement. I have followed much, though not all, of their advice, and I am entirely responsible for the final product. I am most grateful to Lesley Andres, Paul Anisef, William Bruneau, Susan Friedman, Robert Gidney, Marjorie Griffin Cohen, Craig Heron, Ken Hundert, Zeng Lin, Graham Lowe, Wyn Millar, and Lynne Raskin. I would also like to thank Philip Cercone of McGill-Queen's University Press for his enthusiastic support and Carlotta Lemieux for her expert editorial assistance.

Values in Conflict

Introduction

The ground is shifting beneath the contemporary university, and it is time to take stock of its precarious situation. The cultivation of intellect, long a central objective of university life, is threatened by political and economic pressures that are redefining and reshaping the functions of higher learning. In my view, politicians, business leaders, academics, aspiring students, their parents, and the general public need to think critically about these educational directions, and this book, I hope, will contribute to such a discussion.

Universities have a variety of roles, but their most crucial is the nourishing of intellectual life. Once accessible almost exclusively to privileged elites, the academic world is now open to a significantly larger proportion of the population. Yet a variety of forces has conspired to shrink the space that the university provides for fostering the life of the mind. More than ever, higher education is expected to cater directly, quickly, and continually to the demands of the marketplace. In the eyes of many, economic performance, not intellectual enlightenment, is the university's preeminent raison d'être. Similarly, university research that contributes to prescribed commercial purposes earns greater support and recognition than the curiosity-based inquiry that is so central to scholarly independence and the discovery of new knowledge.

Preparing graduates for employment is an undeniable part of the university endeavour, and as I argue in this book, historically it has fulfilled this responsibility fairly well and continues to do so. But in the race for riches, symbolized by endless rhetoric about the need for Canada to become globally competitive, technologically advanced, and proficient at churning out "knowledge workers" for the twenty-first century, something significant is being lost. Our schools and universities are narrowing their educational vistas, and government policy is forcing them to do so. The decision-making autonomy that universities require to fulfill a range of cultural, intellectual, community-service, and training functions is quickly eroding. In particular, liberal education is at risk. In the pages that follow, I hope to demonstrate how this is happening and why it matters.

"Liberal education" is a frequently used but seldom defined concept. It owes its origins to the philosophers and educators of Ancient Greece and Rome; and, remarkably, it has endured for more than two millennia. It is the primary means by which intellectual life has flourished in universities, and over the centuries this has been done in a variety of ways. Indeed, scholars themselves have always disagreed about what liberal education is and how it ought to be pursued, and those debates still carry on. The stated goals of liberal education are sometimes so all-encompassing that everything, including job training and applied research, appear to fall within its domain. This is problematic when universities simultaneously proclaim their undying devotion to the ideals of liberal education while marrying more and more of their academic life to the assumed needs of the marketplace. As they feel compelled to respond to what one author has called the new "economic fundamentalism," universities incrementally marginalize the humanities, the social sciences, and the fine arts.

This is an unusual book for me to have undertaken. As a historian, I most often write about the past, poring over distant experiences that may or may not have left their mark on the present. This volume is more about the future, though history certainly plays an important part in the arguments it makes. Liberal education, whose roots, purposes, and importance are traced in chapters 1 and 2, is not yet dead in the Canadian university. Tenured professors, like me, still have the time and freedom to write books such as this. Undergraduates are still able to major in the liberal arts, and graduate students continue to follow their intellectual interests in the unanticipated directions in which new, stimulating research carries them. But the logic and implications of recent policy, as I contend in chapter 4, do not guarantee that such academic freedoms will endure. It is possible that a decade from now our universities will resemble little more than giant training warehouses, where short-term corporate needs dictate curricula to students who are increasingly taught not by professors but by advanced, impersonal technology. Research, funded primarily by private industry, will be designed to produce profitably-sold products, and will no longer engage the study of non-marketable ideas. "Higher" education will be banal and completely regulated by external authorities. Those interested in exploring the world of ideas might have to set up new institutions (without public funding), perhaps like Plato's Academy, to enable intellectual life to thrive. Some may think that this dystopian vision is already upon us. For the time being, I hold out more hope.

I do not consider that it is wrong for students to view the university as a stepping stone to interesting, relatively secure, and well-paying occupations. Indeed, in chapter 3, I attempt to explain precisely what graduates in the liberal arts and other fields can expect to encounter as they enter the labour market. Nor do I deny the important role universities have in preparing graduates for the labour force. This is a function that they have always carried out, and no realistic observer would expect them to abandon that responsibility. Furthermore, as I argue in chapter 5, there are creative ways of strengthening liberal education and the university as a whole by combining intellectual and employment-based education. But to foster within the university a kind of narrow vocationalism tied to the capricious dictates of the market is exceedingly short-sighted, and it is culturally costly to the individual and society at large. Among other things, it overlooks the fact that the particular intellectual and cultural qualities that liberal education attempts to foster are, directly and indirectly, valuable in virtually all occupations.

Nor do I believe that all of the university's problems are caused by external economic and political forces. To the degree that academics themselves have been dogmatic and intolerant of each other's ideas about liberal education and other university matters, they have generated cynicism among puzzled observers and have undermined their own credibility as teachers and scholars. To the degree that professors make no attempt to appreciate the beliefs and culture of contemporary students or to teach them in more creative ways, they are responsible for alienating at least some of the disenchanted, a theme also explored in chapter 5.

Universities have certainly not escaped the uncertainty of the times, nor should they simply be content to do what they have always done. Indeed, the social, intellectual, and economic roles of higher education have evolved significantly throughout the twentieth century, to say nothing of the changes experienced over the course of the previous millennium. Somehow, the university has managed to balance its various functions so that intellectual life, autonomous scholarly activity, and curiosity-based research in the arts and sciences have survived and thrived. Will this still be the case a generation from now? I am not certain, which is why I have written this book. While it focuses on Canada, it draws from and reflects upon experiences in other countries. It is directed to both academic and non-academic audiences, and is intended to contribute to a dialogue about the importance of cultural life and the pleasures and challenges of exploring ideas. Tomorrow's students are entitled to the kind of education that flows from these tenets. Will they have that opportunity, or will their schooling at all levels simply mirror and reinforce the bottom-line demands of the global economy? In short, how do we and how should we value education?

1
Roots and Branches of Liberal Education

The concept of liberal education is filled with paradox. It is at once the most enduring and changeable of academic traditions. Its roots are in the intellectual culture of Ancient Greece and Rome, and it continues, at least ideally, to embrace some core ideals from that period. At the same time, it has been frequently reinvented over the past two millennia. This chapter surveys the history of various approaches to liberal education, situating the discussion within the context of a broad historical account of higher education itself. This lays the basis for the subsequent discussion of the continuing value of liberal education to contemporary society. But I also acknowledge that the very flexibility of the concept poses some problems. Definitions of liberal education can be overly general, in conflict, or steeped in nostalgia. This chapter traces such expressions and perceptions and leads to what I hope is a more precise and workable definition of liberal education offered in chapter 2.

Most published histories of the Western university begin with a discussion of the educational ideas of the Greek philosophers Socrates and Plato in fifth-century BC and quickly make their way to the founding of Europe's first universities in the twelfth century AD. As I indicate below, any examination of the origins of liberal education must certainly take into account the important events spanning these eras. But higher learning itself has an even longer – and seldom acknowledged – history in the Middle East and Far East.

The Ancient Egyptian kings whose empires featured the great temples of Heliopolis, Karnak, Memphis, and Heracleopolis depended on priests to provide students with religious and practical education in hundreds of temple schools. Privileged cultural elites studied theology, medicine, physics, astronomy, and advanced mathematics, and for some three thousand years these schools served as instruments for securing and transmitting Egypt's cultural heritage. So, too, the Sumerians – who occupied Mesopotamia in the Tigris–Euphrates valley until their fall in 1900 BC – left a literary tramdition as well as scholarship in the sciences and legal studies. Other civilizations in the Fertile Crescent included the Hebrews, who stressed the importance of morality and the centrality of the law of God, which was recorded and interpreted by scribes and scholars.

As early as 1500 BC, near the Indus River Valley in India, the Brahmins, a class of intellectuals and priests, rose to prominence and provided religious and philosophical instruction to select students. By 600 BC, advanced education included the study of philosophy, logic, grammar, and the law, which was offered in *parishads*, university-like institutions in ancient Hindu India. Later, Buddhists and Jainists made higher learning more democratic by opening their monasteries to a wider variety of students, who contributed significantly to Indian cultural and religious life.

In Ancient China, too, scholarly study had an important

place, particularly for state administrators, occupations deemed suitable only for well-educated and morally unimpeachable citizens. From the eighth to the third centuries BC, several schools of thought – Confucianism, Taoism, Moism, and Legalism – vied for students, and intellectual life flourished. Confucianism eventually dominated, and reinforced the role of the scholar as administrator in the country's civil service, a custom that continued into the modern era. Thus, higher learning, largely in pursuit of religious, political, or scientific goals and accessible to small groups of privileged men, was an important part of early oriental history and can scarcely be considered the invention of Western culture.

Still, there are some features of the contemporary university that resonate remarkably with the worlds of Ancient Greece and Rome. By the sixth century BC the Greek city-state, or polis, was a vibrant cosmopolitan and educationally active centre. Pythagoras and his followers lived a "speculative" life and contemplated the abstraction of numbers, thus stimulating interest in the further study of mathematics. With the rise of democracy in the fifth century BC, the Greek city-states (with the exception of Sparta) witnessed the exceptional growth of intellectual life. Ideally, *eleutherios*, or a liberal education, would contribute to the cultivation of the "whole" person, whose "mental, emotional, and bodily parts," potentially at war with one another, would be balanced and integrated.[1] But leading educators advocated different approaches to achieving this goal, thus inspiring one of the first great debates on liberal education. The Sophists focused on the skills that (free) citizens would require to live prosperously in the polis. Offering the subjects of ethics, politics, economics, logic, and rhetoric, the Sophists stressed the importance of perfecting the technique of oral presentation if one hoped to succeed politically. Winning debates by employing rational analysis and speaking with eloquence and conviction seemed essential in a democratic state where voting "determined the outcome of every question arising both in deliberative bodies, which were concerned with making law, and in judicial assemblies where forensic preparations were required."[2]

Socrates (c. 470–399 BC) and his student, Plato (427–347 BC) had different views on the nature of essential learning. They objected to the Sophists' insistence on the educational preeminence of rhetoric. They believed instead in a philosophical approach, through which students would pursue wisdom and truth by disciplining their intellects. In Socrates' view, knowledge, not merely rhetorical skill, was a prerequisite to achieving virtue. Truth might never be found, but the intellectual and moral value of the continual search was incontestable. The "unexamined life," Socrates contended, in a pronouncement that would echo through the ages, "is not worth living for a human being." Plato prescribed a course of study for higher learning that was intended to equip an educated elite to rule society. Steeped in mathematics, dialectics, and metaphysics (philosophy), Plato's followers, some of whom enrolled in the Academy he established in Athens (387 BC), sought to live ethically and philosophically by devoting themselves to the exploration of ideas. Such pursuits, far more than the attainment of "cleverness apart from intelligence and justice,"[3] would, it was hoped, lead to the creation of fully formed and morally sound citizens.

Probably the most influential educator in Ancient Greece was Isocrates (436–338 BC), who leaned towards Sophism but was sceptical of those who used rhetoric simply to get ahead in politics. In his view, the orator, or *rhetor,* ought to be an exemplary citizen who would work for the good of the community. He disagreed both with the importance that Plato and his student Aristotle assigned to mathematics and science and with their determined search for absolute truth. He believed that students should have extensive exposure to literature, poetry, history, music, ethics, and logic. Most importantly, they should apply their intellects and their rhetorical skills to the task of "making wise decisions in the face of limited knowledge." Isocrates believed passionately that higher learning should serve the causes of effective citizenship and strong leadership, which would be facilitated by the study of the classical arts and culture.

In the Hellenistic period (fourth century BC to first century AD), inaugurated by the epochal conquests of Alexander the Great, the polis system waned, and education reflected a mix of Mediterranean and Near Eastern influences. Epicureans and Stoics now stressed the search for individual happiness more than the collective interests of the city-state. In the Museum of Alexandria, scholars pursued scientific inquiry in a range of subject areas, including medicine, astronomy, poetry, and natural history.

When the Romans conquered the Hellenistic East in the second and first centuries BC, they retained their own language of Latin while adopting the educational and cultural practices of the Greeks. The *artes liberales*, a term first believed to have been used by Cicero (106–43 BC), were taught more systematically in the Roman era and were designed to promote patriotism, emphasizing, once again, the importance of rhetoric, or public speech. Cicero intended that each pupil would develop his human capacities to the fullest (*humanitas*), perfecting his speech and reason, as well as his "social, moral and aesthetic instincts."[4] Students were instructed in Latin and Greek, and they studied the work of a variety of writers, including Homer, Plato, Aristotle, Aesop, and Virgil, in addition to the subjects of geography, music, mathematics, geometry, and astronomy. The orator was expected to be a virtuous and ethical leader.

The opportunity to pursue such a course was available only to men enjoying *liberalis,* or freedom. Bruce Kimball suggests that this implied both political freedom (as opposed to slavery) and "the possession of wealth, affording free time for leisure."⁵ Liberal education, therefore, was associated with the perceived social and behavioural qualities of privileged "gentlemen." But like the Greeks, Roman educators were not in complete agreement about which academic subjects mattered most. Followers of Plato stressed the preeminence of philosophy, while rhetoricians emphasized the intellectual and practical value of studying grammar. Such debates would continue well into the future.

Thus, in its earliest incarnation, liberal education appeared to have a number of goals: the cultivation of moral character, intellectual balance and breadth, and commitment to the public good (whose definition flowed from the dominating values of the particular society). Available only to an elite of financially secure males, liberal education was intended to furnish communities with rational and respectable individuals who had the capacity to lead. But conflict infused liberal education from the beginning, as "philosophers" and "orators" clashed over curricular matters, particularly the kind of instruction that would best elevate the intellect and serve the interests of the community.

War, empire building, and the rise of the new religions – Christianity and, later, Islam – consumed the Mediterranean world from the fourth to seventh centuries, when the unity of the region, under Roman rule, ended. The Latin-Germanic West, the Greek-Byzantine East, and the Muslim Middle and Near East competed politically and culturally. Amid continual violence, religious crusades, and economic decline, the Dark Ages left European society, including much of its intellectual life, in a state of decay.

There were, nonetheless, some notable scholarly initiatives. Isidore of Seville (560–636) wrote extensively on the *artes liberales*, stressing the particular importance of literature and grammar over speculative studies, which he feared might lead the reader to question Christian teachings. "Better to be grammarians than heretics," he claimed.[6] This approach foreshadowed the important phase in the history of higher learning in the late Middle Ages (c. 1000–1500) in which Christian theology combined with the Greco-Roman legacy to create a modified version of liberal education and in so doing laid the foundation for the creation of the Western university.

This development owes a good deal to the scholarly contributions of the Islamic world. Having conquered large tracts of territory once held by the Romans, the Muslims had access to the writings of Ancient Greek philosophers, and Muslim scholars proceeded to translate these scripts into Arabic. This work, most significantly that of Aristotle, found its way into Christendom and Western Europe, where it was translated into Latin by bilingual Christians and highly literate Jews who were familiar with Muslim and Christian culture. Notably, Muslim educators also wrote creatively on other subjects, including medicine and philosophy. According to one historian, "the intellectual renaissance of the Latin West in the twelfth and thirteenth centuries would have been impossible without the advances made by the scholars of Islam. Their translations, commentaries, and original speculation on a wide variety of subjects were among the cornerstones of the European curriculum."[7]

This growing cultural interaction was accompanied by an economic revival in Western Europe between the eleventh and thirteenth centuries, which encouraged the development of education. So, too, did the rivalries of European popes, who sought to recruit followers in cathedral schools established in various urban centres. Some of these schools were converted into *studia*, or places of study, where students and masters (teachers) gathered for academic discussions. By the fifteenth century, such an institution was known as a *universitas*, a Latin term that denoted a guild, and in this instance a union of scholars.

Increasingly formalized and strongly influenced by the Roman educational heritage, higher learning in the medieval world was based on the seven liberal arts, divided into the *trivium* (grammar, logic, and rhetoric) and *quadrivium* (mathematics, geometry, astronomy, and music). Upon completion of these courses, the student was awarded a Bachelor of Arts degree, which qualified him to enter the higher faculties of law, medicine, or theology, where he could pursue a master's or doctor's degree.

This structure of the academic hierarchy masked deep debates over theology and philosophy that consumed the intellectual energies of medieval scholars. Faith in God was a given, and the learning of received religious texts was essential. But was there room for critical thinking and analysis within this Catholic intellectual universe? Peter Abelard (1079–1142), a Parisian teacher, thought so. Like some earlier scholars, he considered the study of mathematics to be the foundation for liberal education. The remaining six subjects he subsumed under the study of logic, which he claimed was the essential tool of philosophy. He argued that logic ought to be used in the contemplation of Christian doctrine; in this way, faith could coexist with reason and reflection. He analysed religious and classical texts by positing a *thesis* and *antithesis*, or contrary argument. Some of Abelard's contemporaries disagreed with his approach and sought to silence him by trying him as a heretic who questioned church doctrine.[8]

The access that Christian scholars now had to Greek scholarship, particularly to the voluminous writings of Aristotle, fuelled this scholastic controversy, and Thomas Aquinas (1225–74) attempted to resolve it. He argued that faith and reason were not at odds. Influenced by Aristotelean thinking, he articulated a philosophy of "realism." He saw God at the centre of the universe and held that God's law was more "real" than any individual; that the concept of "law" was more real and enduring than any particular law. Therefore, Christianity could be embraced, even as some of its self-proclaimed spokespersons (corrupt popes, for example) could be rejected. Such logic and critical reasoning, however, required a most disciplined, philosophically sound mind. Aquinas helped to expand intellectual discourse, even though many Christians never embraced his eclectic thinking. University curricula, though, did tend to reflect his influence. Philosophy was added to the liberal arts program as a discrete subject and was divided into three categories – natural philosophy, moral philosophy, and metaphysics. By the end of the Middle Ages, liberal education at Oxford, Paris, and Salamanca was unquestionably still rooted in Christian theology but was inspired by the Christian scholars' Greek forebears: the critic and the rationalist had a distinctive if tenuous place in the university.

Women, it should be noted, had virtually no place in scholarly life. This was not always the case in Christendom. In the seventh century, some had belonged to "double" monasteries, and coeducation was not unusual, particularly for intellectually ambitious noblewomen. During the Crusades, however, when militaristic values mixed with religious ones, notions of aggressive masculinity characterized the spirit of the age, and women increasingly were excluded from public life and confined to domestic roles. From Aristotle (who viewed women as "defective males") to St Paul, to Aquinas, scholars and religious authorities justified the exclusion of women from higher learning and reinforced the concept of liberal education – signified by a "bachelor's" degree – as a "gentlemanly" or clerical prerogative.[9]

By 1500 there were seventy-two universities in Europe, but doctrinal conflicts within the Catholic Church and continuing battles between church and state, into which professors were drawn, fuelled disenchantment with the condition of higher education. Scholasticism, the assiduous study of religious and selected classical texts, appeared to many to have lost its creative thrust, serving the cause of religious orthodoxy far more than genuine higher learning.

Among the leading critics were Renaissance scholars, particularly in fourteenth- and fifteenth-century Italy, who sought to decouple classical studies from Christian theology. Reflecting a more dynamic and at times even rebellious age, they championed *studia humanitatis*, which gave preeminence to those subjects that explored the human condition. They were inspired by Ancient Greek and Roman classical writing, which they believed had been inappropriately distorted by medieval scholastics in order to serve religious purposes. Higher learning, they contended, ought to encourage greater individualism and a wider range of literary forms, including essays, biography, and poetry. While some existing universities were open to these intellectual challenges, many weren't, leading to the establishment of some new, alternative institutions, such as the Platonic Academy in Florence in the late fifteenth century.

Only gradually, and only in the more liberally minded institutions, did the "humanistic" studies become integrated into the university curriculum. To the degree that the Renaissance writers rearticulated classical ideals of the well-spoken, intellectually refined citizen-scholar, they contributed little that was new to the world of scholarship. But they did serve as a catalyst to the spread of an important dimension of liberal education that was partly comprehended later in the Enlightenment and was more fully embraced in the twentieth-century university: the need for scholarship to be free from unreasonable restraints and to be liberated to explore the full range of human beliefs and actions. With the invention of movable type in 1454, which facilitated the dissemination of knowledge in unprecedented forms, these prospects were considerably enhanced.

The tension between theologically based higher learning and

the spirit of critical inquiry continued from the sixteenth to nineteenth centuries and spread to North America. One response to Catholic dominance of higher education flowed from the Reformation movement, spearheaded by the German monk Martin Luther (1483–1546), who challenged the authoritarianism and political "hypocrisy" of traditional religious establishments. His Protestant followers now claimed to be the true messengers of Christ's word, and they established universities throughout Europe and eventually the British colonies in order to restore religious piety and train their own clergy. Led by the Jesuit Order, Catholics responded with the Counter-Reformation, building a host of colleges, universities, and seminaries throughout the world, including one at Quebec in 1635.

Notwithstanding their doctrinal differences, traditional study prevailed in Catholic and Protestant institutions alike. Greek and Latin classics were core subjects, in which students were required to be fluent. Not unlike medieval scholastics, theological instruction consumed academic life. University teaching was generally regimented and demanding, and in its attention to textual detail it contributed, at its best, to a traditional goal of liberal education – the disciplining of the mind. But it largely failed to engage with emerging fields of intellectual inquiry.

Enlightenment scholars in the seventeenth and eighteenth centuries – those devoted to scientific exploration, rationality, scepticism, and the concept of human progress – had some influence on academic life, but Christian higher learning was essentially hostile to the secularizing implications of much Enlightenment thinking. Galileo (1564–1642), an astronomer and physicist, was expelled from an Italian university, condemned by the Inquisition in Rome, and compelled to recant his "error in philosophy" for supporting the Copernican theory that the sun, not the earth, was the centre of the universe.

The work of René Descartes (1596–1650) in philosophy and mathematics was circulated in academies and research centres *outside* universities. Nor were the French *philosophes*, whose ideas on liberty and equality proved eventually to be so influential, employed in universities. On the other hand, Isaac Newton (1642–1727), later considered one of the world's most accomplished scientists, taught at Cambridge from 1669 to 1701 and was received more favourably in the academic world. The University of Halle in Germany, founded in 1737, allowed professors to lecture in German, to separate the study of theology from that of philosophy, and to pursue scholarship more freely than was customary. Scottish universities were especially open to newer philosophical perspectives by such thinkers as David Hume (1711–76), whose sceptical thinking challenged both theological and more recent materialist ideas about the nature of reality. The venerable Oxford University in England, by contrast, more resolutely upheld intellectual and academic traditions, remaining wedded to the visions and practices of the Church of England.

The nineteenth century witnessed extensive intellectual and institutional changes in the development of higher education. Church-led higher educational institutions endured, especially in North America, but state-funded, nondenominational universities and colleges spread rapidly throughout Europe and the United States, and to a lesser extent in England. In an era of intense nationalistic rivalries, higher education, more than ever, was intended to serve the cause of nation building, both in the highly centralized systems of France and Germany and in the relatively decentralized American and Canadian systems.

In the German case, particularly at Humboldt University (established in 1809), two cornerstones of contemporary university life were legitimated: specialized research and academic freedom. The latter permitted students and faculty to pursue scholarly life unimpeded, so long as they did not act in politically subversive ways by challenging the authority of the state. Thus the liberty that liberal (and other) educators enjoyed was simultaneously unprecedented and still highly conditional. Specialized research in Germany inspired scholarly work elsewhere, especially in science, and influenced the development of graduate study in the United States.

The tendency towards academic specialization also affected undergraduates, particularly in the wake of the new "elective system" established at Harvard University in the 1870s by President Charles W. Eliot, an initiative that renewed debates about the nature of liberal education. Harvard dramatically reduced the number of compulsory courses, freeing undergraduate students to structure their courses of study from among a range of academic fields. Eliot and his followers believed that knowledge could not be contained within traditional philosophical and pedagogical parameters and that academics, including students, would contribute to higher learning and their own intellectual development by exercising academic choices responsibly. Furthermore, intellectual depth required scholars to probe a single subject deeply, and America's industrial progress demanded a more pertinent, socially applicable form of higher education than that traditionally provided by the mandatory study of religion and the classics. Eliot's belief that liberal studies should liberate the intellect "in an atmosphere of freedom"[10] challenged "the classical notion of a liberal education ... in which truth was looked upon as uniform, fixed and eternal."[11]

Eliot's critics, most notably, James McCosh, the president of Princeton, deplored what they viewed as the fragmentation and moral disorder flowing from such forms of undergraduate education. They contended, too, that professional training and specialized research eroded the core purpose of higher education: the cultivation of virtue and character through exemplary teaching. Surely, the latter would serve the national interest better than unguided study or research on minor or voguish social questions. They agreed with the British critic Matthew Arnold (1822–88), who claimed that the purpose of liberal education was to connect students to their cultural heritage by teaching "the best that is known and thought in the world."[12]

This intellectual struggle between the so-called "Ancients and the Moderns"[13] was deepened by the conflict over Darwinian science in the last half of the nineteenth century. In what many religious scholars considered a presumptuous and false proposition, Charles Darwin (1809–82), an English naturalist, contended that all species, including humans, evolved, changed, or disappeared according to observable laws of nature. This idea challenged the theory of creationism and biblical authority itself, and inspired further scientific research that explained reality without direct reference to the role of God. Some scholars sought to reconcile intellectually scientific and spiritual principles, but this balance was difficult to sustain in a world captivated by medical and technological innovations (electricity, for example) that exhibited the power of emerging research and experimentation.[14] By the end of the century, the theory of evolution was being commonly taught in universities throughout Europe and North America.

A poignant illustration of both the development and the paradoxes of liberal education is the work of Cardinal John Henry Newman (1801–90), an English churchman and scholar who wrote influentially on higher education in the mid-nineteenth century. An Anglican convert to Catholicism, he believed that students required an orthodox Christian education in order to develop fully their moral sensibilities. Secure in their faith, students should also be exposed to knowledge arising from the secular world, including the study of literature, philosophy, history, and science. With the "Moderns," he celebrated the liberated intellect and claimed, "Knowledge is capable of being its own end."[15] At the same time he believed that liberal education had a distinctive social purpose, designed to shape the characters of selected individuals: "Liberal education makes not the Christian, nor the Catholic, but the gentleman. It is well to have a cultivated intellect, a delicate taste, a candid, equitable, dispassionate mind, a noble and courteous bearing in the conduct of life – these are the connatural qualities of large knowledge; they are the objects of a University."[16]

By the beginning of the twentieth century, liberal education was intent less on perpetuating Christian doctrine than on preparing "gentlemen" for their appropriate social roles. The wealth of new knowledge, in part, led to this change. So did the emerging system of industrial capitalism, which required a wider range of professionally educated graduates who could minister to the needs of private corporations, the public service, and the expanding school populations. In the English-speaking world, the study of English replaced religion and the classics as a core subject; the latter survived in nondenominational universities as course options or specialized topics, along with other humanities and social science subjects. The humanities included English, history, philosophy, religion, languages (ancient and modern), and the fine arts. The social sciences, no longer adequately contained within the nineteenth-century subject of moral philosophy, consisted of psychology, economics, political science, geography, anthropology, and, increasingly, sociology.

Most institutions retained the traditional goal of requiring students to have intellectual "breadth," but the curricular components of typical courses of study looked much different than they had a generation earlier. Students "concentrated" on, or majored in, a particular subject and broadened their education by selecting courses from other subject areas. Notwithstanding these changes, an undergraduate education still claimed to be capable of effectively moulding individual character by imbuing the student with sound morals, civility, and the spirit of patriotism. It would provide a necessary foundation for professional training and exemplary occupational performance. It would help elevate culture and prepare society's leaders. Mirroring the economic world that graduates were preparing to enter, the university increasingly resembled a vast marketplace of ideas and activities. Liberal education was now an important instrument of the university's broader function – equipping mostly middle-class youth for respectable and prestigious positions in middle-class communities.[17]

The emphasis on the preparation of "gentlemen" masks another important change in the evolution of the university – the admission of women. The debate over this question was particularly intense during the 1870s, though echoes of it continued well into the next century. In opposing coeducation, Edward Clarke, a Harvard medical professor, combined religious faith with an idiosyncratic version of evolutionary theory. He claimed that "identical education of the sexes is a crime before God and humanity ... which emasculates boys and stunts girls."[18] Supporters of this view feared that under the pressures of university examinations, women would damage themselves physically and mentally, possibly even threatening their reproductive capacities, a problem somehow not associated with the demands of domestic work, for which women were considered naturally suited.

While some proponents of higher education for women stressed the theme of gender equality, most, especially male educators, did not. They argued that because middle-class women occupied a "separate sphere" in society – a nurturing role at home and in the community – the university could enhance this capacity if it educated them appropriately. Thus, once women were admitted to North American universities, generally in the 1870s and 1880s, they typically studied in the humanities and the fine arts, not in the sciences, social sciences, or professional fields such as medicine and law. Rather than using higher education to prepare her for long-term employment, the female student was expected to cultivate her linguistic or artistic capacities, her ability to carry on intelligent discussion, and her organizational skills so that she might perform effectively as a community volunteer. A university-educated woman, furthermore, ought to be "a fit companion for a wiser and nobler man, than she otherwise would have been."[19] By the early twentieth century, then, a university-based liberal arts education could help prepare women, as well as men, for culturally acceptable but different roles within middle-class communities. A generation earlier, in a more austere academic climate, such a notion would have been dismissed as heretical or revolutionary.

As we have seen, innovative ideas in one period become the prevailing orthodoxy in subsequent eras, a pattern well illustrated by the history of competing visions of liberal education. The American-inspired elective system, which embraced the principle of curricular choice, elicited growing criticism in the years following World War I. While some believed that the university had become merely an academic free-for-all, catering without discrimination to every intellectual and social whim, others, such as American educational philosopher John Dewey (1859–1952), felt that the problem of academic fragmentation flowed from the dramatic and relentless expansion of knowledge in the arts and sciences. A proposed solution – "general" and "integrated" education – drew conceptually from the past. Academic coherence was sought first through new compulsory survey courses in the various disciplines, intended to ground students intellectually before they chose their subjects of specialization. Robert Hutchins, president of the University of Chicago from 1929 to 1945, considered survey courses a small but still inadequate step towards restoring unity and order to liberal education. Encouraged by initiatives

at Columbia University and St John's College, he endorsed the
Great Books approach, designed to introduce students to some
hundred "essential" texts that would make liberal education
genuinely achievable. Echoing the views of Matthew Arnold,
he wrote: "Education implies teaching. Teaching implies
knowledge. Knowledge is truth. The truth is everywhere the
same. Hence education should be everywhere the same."[20]
Critics would subsequently challenge both Hutchins's belief in
the universality of knowledge and truth, and the dilettantism
allegedly fostered by the Great Books approach itself. Furthermore, its prescription of classical, English, and American texts
aroused the complaint, in a later generation, that liberal education via the Great Books was culturally exclusive and was
condescending to the experiences of non-Western communities, racial minorities, and women.

Led by the example of the University of Toronto, which
itself was inspired by the "Oxford mystique," many English
Canadian universities sought to preserve the integrity of liberal education by creating two academic streams: pass (or general) courses, and an elite honours degree in which students
would specialize intensively in a single subject with scarcely
any course options. Ideally, then, honours courses would meet
the demand for specialization while preserving a common
course of study for the most gifted students.[21]

Liberal arts education as a whole was threatened in Canada
(and Britain) by the demands imposed on universities by
World War II. The armed forces craved graduates from science, engineering, and medicine, and Canadian universities
answered the call by moving academic resources into these
fields and away from the humanities, which according to the
principal of Queen's University were in "eclipse." His propos-
al to the National Conference of Canadian Universities (sub-
mitted with the principal of McGill) to suspend all teaching in
"non-essential" academic fields (i.e., the arts) was repudiated

and successfully resisted by other Canadian academics, who argued that the war was being fought against tyrants who had no use for intellectual autonomy and democratic living – principles intrinsic to liberal arts education.[22]

Indeed, as the curriculum grew over the course of the twentieth century – driven by secularization, specialization, and professionalization – the worlds of the sciences and arts became increasingly isolated within the university. In the United States, as Frederick Rudolph explains, the advocates of liberal culture in the early 1900s stressed "art, literature, history and philosophy. Liberal culture was unwilling to bring science within its understanding or under its influence" because science was perceived by many in the humanities to be exceedingly narrow in its orientation and application.[23] Notwithstanding the Great Books and other general education initiatives designed to restore coherence and breadth in the curriculum, the cultural rift between the arts and sciences remained and, arguably, intensified.

In Canada – partly because of limited resources – arts and science were typically offered within the same ("Arts and Science") faculties, and until at least the 1960s, arts students were required, usually in first year, to take one course in science, while science students were compelled to enrol in one or two arts courses. But, at best, these fields coexisted rather than interacting. Because of the "crucial importance of the practical applications of scientific activity in the prosecution of the [World War II] effort,"[24] science was subsequently associated – accurately or not – with applied, pragmatic purposes, while the arts were the presumed means by which students were liberally and more broadly educated. As we shall see later, there have been renewed efforts in recent years to reintegrate the disciplines – and reinvigorate liberal education – through such vehicles as "liberal science" programs.

By the end of World War II, no single version of liberal education successfully imposed itself on North American and European universities. Pushed by external economic and social forces, and forever immersed in internal intellectual debates, universities continually modified their missions and mandates, and eclecticism was the order of the day. The goals of liberal education had expanded, and universities attempted to make a virtue from this apparent necessity. As Bruce Kimball notes, liberal education in American institutions "affirmed diversity but called for unity; offered breadth and eschewed superficiality; extolled freedom and called for discipline; proclaimed democratic equality while demanding standards; honored individuality beside social responsibility; hailed intellectual along with spiritual, emotional and physical development; promised a 'foundation on which to base ... occupational activities,' but not vocational education; and recognized that no idea of liberal education is final but expected students to find a firm philosophy of life."[25]

This pattern of meeting growing demands accelerated in the post–World War II era. In the 1950s, during the Cold War, the social sciences and humanities were intended, on the one hand, to promote the values of intellectual freedom and democracy and, on the other hand, to prevent the expression of "subversive" ideas, especially though not only in the United States.[26] Student protests during the 1960s resurrected the campaign for curricular choice and freedom of expression, and eventually succeeded in throwing off the last vestiges of *in loco parentis*, by which university authorities had served as students' moral guardians. In nondenominational universities, undergraduates typically achieved unprecedented degrees of autonomy in curricular and extracurricular areas, though religious colleges were still inclined to regulate student life in traditionally paternalistic ways. Student reformers also demanded that the social sciences and humanities address "relevant" community concerns. Liberal education, from this perspective, should contribute to social progress, particularly to the achievement of greater social equality. Radicals condemned the university's alleged complicity in the conduct of war, in perpetuating social class and racial privilege, and in ministering uncritically to private corporate interests. Interestingly, many activists challenged the principle that university courses should explore ideas for their own sake, a previously innovative concept now deemed by such critics to be elitist and socially irresponsible.[27]

Driven by demographic pressures, the economic demand for well-educated graduates, and the public belief that higher education was the route to a secure and rewarding life, university enrolments expanded significantly from the 1960s to the 1980s, especially in North America. The scope of higher education broadened yet again, and the tendency to curricular specialization escalated. In the humanities and social sciences, students could choose from an almost bewildering range of courses. In addition to the now traditional disciplines (history, sociology, English, etc.), multi- and interdisciplinary programs emerged in such areas as communications, urban studies, cultural studies, women's studies, and multicultural studies.

The latter subjects arose from intensive campaigns on university campuses in favour of social "equity," and amid the so-called culture wars of the 1980s and 1990s, academics battled again around the issue of curricular reform. On one side were those lamenting the modern, especially the post-modern, direction of the liberal arts. With the late University of Chicago scholar Allan Bloom, who wrote the best-selling book, *The Closing of the American Mind* (1987), they deplored the specialization, fragmentation, and politicization of the curriculum, especially the incursion into universities of "identity" politics, based on the divisive issues of gender and race. The campus confrontations arising from the turbulent 1960s had, according to Bloom, further compromised the integrity of liberal education and the university's role in the preservation of high culture. Liberal arts programs used to require students to study the classics, English literature, and the towering figures of Western thought, but this had given way to a curricular smorgasbord, without coherence or acceptable standards, thriving within an anti-intellectual university. The "crisis of liberal education," argued Bloom, was "a reflection of ... the crisis of our civilization."[28]

Critics of this perspective were scarcely silent. In *The Opening of the American Mind*, Lawrence W. Levine challenged the thin research, historical distortions, and ideological partisanship of a number of publications opposing curricular revision. The growing presence on university campuses of women and students from diverse cultural and racial groups was bound to affect curricular life, and Levine argued that it was precisely the fields of social history, multiculturalism, and women's studies that introduced students to traditionally marginalized peoples and to previously invisible worlds, thus strengthening liberal education by pushing back the frontiers of knowledge. Indeed, Martha C. Nussbaum found justification for the new curriculum in the Socratic tradition itself, which stressed not only the centrality of the "examined life" but also, in the hands of the Stoics, its "pluralism," in that it explored different cultural traditions.[29] Ironically, as noted earlier, had it not been for a form of multiculturalism in the Middle Ages, in which Arab translators made the work of the Ancient Greeks accessible to European scholars, the first Western "classics" might itself still be unknown.

Whatever the protagonists' intellectual merits (explored further in chapter 2), the debates about liberal education were at times conducted illiberally and were fuelled by other controversial issues such as affirmative-action hiring and sexual harassment policies.[30] If liberal education were to thrive in the contemporary university, it appeared to require a more consistently dispassionate and civil discourse, and a meaningful affirmation of the principle of intellectual tolerance. Academic approaches from the past and present had much to contribute to these discussions. It remained to be seen, at the dawn of the new millennium, whether scholars, let alone university funders and policy makers, were prepared to take up this vital challenge.

Indeed, external patrons, private corporations, government spokespersons, and the public at large appeared preoccupied with a single aspect of higher education – the pragmatic, professional, and career-training dimension. As I suggested earlier, one of the enduring historical debates in the life of the university has turned on the importance of professional training and the influence of the marketplace on liberal education. There are many examples of academic battles on this question between those favouring the religious, moral, or cultural purposes of liberal education and those stressing its applied, utilitarian function. Egerton Ryerson, Ontario's superintendent of education from 1844 to 1876, believed that the university should provide "mental discipline fundamentally rooted in social memory," while Daniel Wilson, the president of the University of Toronto, believed that universities should be more effectively "fitting men for the actual business of life."[31] The American economist and social critic Thorstein Veblen believed that by 1900 the American university was dominated and damaged by business and professional interests, a sentiment shared by Canadian historian Frank Underhill, who accused engineering schools of doing little more than producing "barbarians who can build bridges."[32]

As I argue later in this book, there are good reasons to worry about the impact of market values and market forces on higher education, particularly on the liberal arts. But those of us taking this position should also acknowledge the complementary, or at least symbiotic, nature of the historical relationship between the economic and cultural dimensions of university life. The universities of the Middle Ages trained not only ministers but also lawyers, judges, accountants, administrators, and doctors, who used the liberal education subjects of logic and oratory to conduct the business of the churches, the diplomatic service, and the civil state. The industrial era of the nineteenth and early twentieth centuries, which unquestionably drew the university further into the marketplace by preparing middle-class professionals, also coincided with and to some degree inspired the emergence of the social sciences, which engaged academics in the study of human affairs in an increasingly urban, secular world.

Consider as well the impressive expansion of the liberal arts during the period of massive university growth in Canada (and elsewhere) between 1960 and 1970. Inspired by a belief in the value of human capital, politicians, businessmen, and educators could justify spending on virtually all aspects of higher education, which by definition was expected to contribute to the nation's burgeoning wealth. Within certain limits, universities generally had the autonomy (and the funding) required to determine their own educational priorities, and as enrolment patterns indicated, the arts were high on most institutions' curricular lists. The liberal arts and the faculty employed to teach them had benefited, at least indirectly, from a prevailing popular belief in the job-training function of higher education.[33] And it would be naive of academics today to assume that universities would be supported or enrolled at current levels if the institutions were stripped of their economic role in favour of an exclusively cultural one.

Thus, to the multitude of liberal education's goals we should add the most utilitarian one: preparation of students for the workforce. Furthermore, proponents of this priority can defend it in terms familiar both to traditional and modern advocates of the liberal arts. Does responsible citizenship not require gainful employment? Does fulfilling one's creative potential and developing the "whole" person not demand a meaningful occupational outlet for the knowledge acquired in university? From this perspective, the needs of the market, perhaps more than ever in this age of economic uncertainty, should shape the university curriculum. Arguably, given their malleability and breadth, the principles of liberal education would not be compromised by this approach.

But this is precisely the seductive investment-based thinking, taken to extreme, that exposes most of the liberal arts to danger. When market priorities and demands dominate university life, can there be room for "pure" scholarship and teaching in an environment bereft of adequate resources? If university courses cannot be justified on obvious utilitarian grounds, will they be protected? Will intellectual initiatives that generate insufficient funding, low enrolments, or limited employment prospects be possible? Given recent policy trends in Canada and abroad (discussed in chapter 4), there are indeed grounds for concern. As Sheldon Rothblatt notes, "The desire to turn liberal education into an article of private consumption, which individualist and relatively wealthy societies permit, thwarts [its] larger purpose but is itself able to draw on historical sources of support and justification."[34]

Partly by design, partly unintentionally, and clearly the result of its complex history, liberal education today serves a wide range of goals that arise from academic, cultural, community-based, political, and economic forces. The debates among rival proponents of these aims continue. For some, this is evidence of a university that has lost its way and is riven with intellectual chaos in a time of dissolving social consensus about education and most other matters, leading to what the late Bill Readings has called "a university in ruins."[35]

Yet Readings's interpretation of this state is less despairing than one might have expected. He argued that the university's

inability to resolve internal philosophical and academic differences is the very source of its enduring vitality and importance. Comprising of so many constituencies and visions, the
university "community is not organic in that its members do
not share an immanent identity to be revealed; the community is not directed toward the production of a universal subject
of history, to the cultural realization of an essential human
nature."[36] The curricular, theological, or ideological uniformity that characterized liberal education in earlier eras can no
longer be sustained within the university. But members of the
community *are* obligated to continue their scholarly ventures,
and they depend on one another to facilitate this process.
They do not necessarily pursue the same goals, but they are
members of a community with an identifiable purpose: "The
University is where thought takes place beside thought, where
thinking is a shared process without identity or unity."[37] One
might infer that threats to the existence of one constituency,
arising from ideological dogmatism or economic expediency,
pose a threat to all. As I will argue in the next chapter, liberal
education, reconsidered in light of this reality, still plays an
essential role in the life of the mind, the university, and the
community at large.

2
Intellect, Culture, and Community

Historically, liberal education has been the foundation of academic life, yet it defies easy categorization and definition. In the face of such conceptual uncertainty in an era of volatile change, is an unambiguous, intellectually sound meaning of liberal education possible and defensible? I believe it is, and this chapter endeavours to provide it. The proposed definition attempts to reflect the traditions and dynamism of liberal education and to indicate its continuing academic and social value. It seeks to avoid intellectual nostalgia and is informed by current academic and cultural realities. I hope to demonstrate that the continual devaluing of liberal education will be costly to students and to the communities where they choose to live and work.

Liberal education in the university refers to activities that are designed to cultivate intellectual creativity, autonomy, and resilience; critical thinking; a combination of intellectual breadth and specialized knowledge; the comprehension and

*tolerance of diverse ideas and experiences; informed partici-
pation in community life; and effective communication skills.*
While usually associated with teaching and research in the
humanities and the social sciences (generally deemed the "liberal arts"), these objectives can and should be integrated into
scientific, technical, and professional education. In this chapter and again in chapter 5, I will provide examples of the ways
in which liberal education can both enrich and profit from
academic initiatives that seek to integrate (rather than isolate)
the arts, the sciences, vocational training, and the professions.

These elements of liberal education both echo the past and
situate themselves in the present. Intellectual resilience, for
example, was expected from orators and philosophers, from
theologians and Renaissance poets, from the generally educated and the specialist researchers. But the tolerance of
diversity is a more contemporary educational ideal and, as I
contend below, an essential one. The goal of fostering
communication skills will strike some liberal educators as
crass and unduly vocationalist. I believe, however, that from
Plato's day onward, liberal education has embraced this principle, even if it has been described in more refined (or more
pretentious) terms.

Creativity, Autonomy, Resilience

If the goals of cultivating creativity, autonomy, and intellectual resilience seem almost too self-evident to merit discussion,
we should remember that this was not always the case. When
liberal educators sought to imbue "gentlemen" with religious
virtue, as in the Middle Ages, or with "the best that is known
and thought," as in the mid-nineteenth century, they did not
necessarily cherish creative thinking or even intellectual
autonomy in their students; to be liberally educated was to
absorb the scriptures or the classics and to think and reason

within clearly prescribed paradigms. Students educated well in these circumstances knew a great deal, were multilingual, and could conduct sophisticated theological discussions, but they were taught that certain ideas and knowledge – Darwinism, for example – were dangerous and, if believed, could lead to intellectual and moral anarchy. Liberal education was as much about containing thought as about disseminating knowledge.[1]

Liberal education today stresses the liberating rather than prophylactic value of higher learning. Some private evangelical Bible colleges, particularly in the United States, may still cling to a traditional notion of liberal education by attempting to protect their students, both in the curriculum and the extracurriculum, from the forces of "secular humanism," but most liberal educators encourage students to think more creatively and independently, and favour what Charles Anderson calls the "intrinsic" purpose of the university, which is "to find out what can be done with the powers of the mind."[2]

There ought to be as few restrictions as possible in such educational pursuits, though the student's ability to undertake autonomous intellectual inquiry is not innate or automatic; he or she requires careful direction. A political science major interested in the topic of anarchy, for example, would be encouraged by a responsible instructor to explore the subject deeply. The student would be expected to explain and define the concept, including competing versions of it, research its origins, probe its theoretical strengths and weaknesses, examine it in practice, and, finally, assess its virtues. If successfully written, such an essay would move the student from the realms of ignorance, personal opinion, or impression to informed understanding. He or she would grapple with conflicting ideas and evidence, and would, independently, come to a meaningful conclusion. The most creative student would offer an original interpretive insight, perhaps laying the basis for additional study.

Of course, the student could not begin such research without some intellectual foundation, Presumably, a background course (possibly compulsory) in the development of political thought, in which various political ideologies were compared and explained, would have laid the basis for such an essay. It might even have piqued the student's interest in the specific subject of anarchy. Thus, for the student to be equipped to engage in autonomous work, he or she requires the university to convey the knowledge it has about the disciplines it offers. Professors do this not to provide final answers for the questions they explore, but to present a kind of progress report on the state of the scholarship, to demonstrate the importance of organized and coherent thought, and to offer students the prospect of refining their own thinking on issues that interest them. As Anderson notes, "The process of thought is open, unpredictable, unbounded ... For this reason the products of the university are always imperfect and provisional ... The moral of this, of course, is that the university always understands its teaching is improvised, that it always keep working on schemes of reason, never entrench them as dogma ... The basic work of the university is to create systems of reason, practices of inquiry."[3]

Ideally, students who master the practice of reasoned inquiry will continue to use it as members of the community. Of course, they will be unlikely to write any more essays – unless they pursue graduate work or writing careers – but they may well have learned some valuable skills: to think clearly for themselves, to distinguish thoughtlessness and dogma from informed opinion and argument, and to make judgments carefully and, eventually, decisively. Perhaps they will also have developed an enduring appreciation for the world of ideas and for continuing education itself, which they will pass on to others. As James O. Freedman writes, "A liberal education ... stirs students to probe the mysteries of the natural world, to reflect on the rise and fall of cultures, to find meaning in the enduring achievements of Western and Eastern civilizations, and to consider ambiguities and arguable lessons of human history. Further, a liberal education encourages students to seek the affirmation of their most authentic selves. It sets in motion a process of critical examination and imaginative introspection that leads students towards personal definition. It helps students develop an independent perspective for reflecting on the nature and texture of their lives ... [and] conveys ... a sense of joy in learning – joy in participating in the life of the mind."[4]

Critical Thinking

Contemporary academics commonly extol the virtues and centrality of critical thinking in liberal education, something their predecessors would have been less inclined to do. This is not to say that scholarly life in earlier generations lacked introspection or vigorous debate, but these practices were largely the prerogative of faculty rather than students. Determined to cultivate piousness, patriotism, respectability, and intellectual conformity to dominant ideas, universities may have tolerated but would not have encouraged dissidence and criticism among students. Those engaged in professional and other forms of educational training were particularly subjected to a pedagogy that required the accumulation of received factual knowledge and allegiance to known systems of practice. Indeed, the professional education of doctors, lawyers, clergy, *and* academics involved a process of socialization to values that helped make higher education a pillar of social order well into the twentieth century.[5]

We now live in an era in which critical thinking, arguably, has moved from the fringes of the higher educational process to occupy a central place in the instructional mission. As suggested in the previous chapter, the combination of influential social movements since the 1960s, the continuing explosion of knowledge, the rapid pace of social change, and the growing uncertainty about intellectual matters – and about the direction of society itself – have contributed to this development. So, too, has the contemporary university's virtual abandonment of its role as the student's moral guardian. Liberal educators expect students to reason their own ways to knowledge and understanding, aided but not coerced by professors.

Critical thinking, effectively learned, ought to provide students with an ability to assess the legitimacy of competing ideas, both inside and outside the university. In an era in which the effective manipulation of new media influences public opinion, including the outcome of contests for political power, society requires citizens who are sceptical of rhetoric and informed about important public issues. Jansen and van der Veen contend that in the face of a technology-driven, ecologically disturbed, and economically polarized world, major social, political, and ethical questions face every society, and the issue of the quality of leadership is especially pressing. "Who should rule us, who should manage us, how should we control them, are questions that have to be posed again and now on a much broader, global scale," and by enabling students to probe such matters intensively, liberal education, directly and indirectly, has a vital role to play in helping society answer these questions.[6]

Critical thinking, in an academic context, however, does not mean merely learning to criticize. Indeed, if one challenges an idea without a sophisticated understanding of the idea itself, then one risks articulating thought superficially. Certain facts must be learned, in any field of study, to build a solid intellectual foundation, including the building of a critical perspective. As Anderson argues, a professor is ill advised to begin a course by attacking conventional theories in order to introduce students quickly to an alternative perspective or paradigm. Students should first understand established ideas in their social and historical context and be encouraged to examine fully the contemporary value of such views. Playing devil's advocate by arguing a position in opposition to one's own perspective is a useful exercise for professors and students. Doing so enables one to grasp how "practice developed historically out of a process of deliberate, evolutionary effort to resolve the puzzles and paradoxes, the limitations, of earlier usages and understandings."[7] Once the student demonstrates an informed understanding of traditional theory, he or she can begin to question its continuing relevance. If the student – and professor – subsequently do adopt a critical perspective, the same rules apply. It must intellectually withstand criticism and must be subjected to the same type of scrutiny as the approach(es) it replaced.

But a critical appreciation of an idea or theory does not require one to reject it. The student may favour capital punishment both before and after researching and debating the subject in the classroom but may come away from the discussion with a more profound understanding of why she holds this view. Is it founded on reason, emotion, evidence, socialization (i.e., parental influence), religious faith, or a combination of all of these forces? Having addressed the matter in this way, the student would presumably be in a better position to judge the basis of, and participate in, public debate on the same issue. Such a process of questioning could either reinforce or unsettle the student's world view. At any rate, her self-knowledge would grow, owing in part to the process of rational inquiry arising from liberal learning. Recalling Socrates, the philosopher Mark Kingwell contends that "we must examine our beliefs, not merely hold them. Critical reflection comes inevitably in the wake of trying to give reasons for why we do things, and this reflection is, importantly, internal to the social practice in which it appears."[8]

Critical thinking, and thus liberal education itself, can be compromised by forces that erode the autonomy of the student, or the professor. Teachers – including those in the liberal arts – who tolerate no questioning of their own ideas, or who demean those students who express alternative views, diminish the educational experience. So does teaching that fails to help students make the transition from fact learning to conceptualization. Similarly, academic researchers – in the arts and sciences – who skew their scholarship to serve the interests of funding sponsors threaten the integrity of the university by surrendering their intellectual autonomy to influential patrons. The *New England Journal of Medicine* found in 1998 that researchers who received grants from the pharmaceutical industry were far more likely to endorse company products than those who obtained research funds from nonindustry agencies. The absence of critical perspective in such cases, possibly motivated by self-interest, "has the potential to prejudice the objectivity of [the researchers'] results."[9] The more prevalent such practices, the more sullied is the quality of higher learning.

Breadth and Specialization

Educators have long debated the degree to which undergraduate education should promote "general" knowledge or more intensive specialized study. In eras when all students studied the same subjects in a common curriculum, general education held sway. Steeped in the trivium (expression) and quadrivium (arts and science), the medieval learner was taught all that was deemed worth knowing. Armed with such knowledge, he would, ideally, be equipped to contribute in esteemed ways to

religious and other aspects of community life. While the ora-
torical and philosophical traditions stressed different aspects
of the curriculum, they shared an interest in cultivating the
student's moral development and exposing him to the presumed totality of intellectual life. In an era when books were
few and far between, this was a reasonable ambition.

Renaissance and Enlightenment thinkers, however, were
increasingly inclined to equate liberal education with "freedom and open-mindedness," and to encourage the search for
new knowledge, particularly in the sciences and philosophy.[10]
Industrialization was accompanied by the emergence of new
professions and the demand for more diverse and specialized
education. As discussed in the previous chapter, the contest in
higher education was thus engaged between generalists who
deplored the erosion of a unified curriculum and specialists
who favoured intensive research and more academic choice
for students.

Such arguments have persisted to the present day. Echoing
Cardinal John Henry Newman, Joseph Wagner, for example,
laments "the lack of shared commitments, an atrophy of
common values, [and] a deterioration of community" in the
university, caused mainly by an "inappropriate emphasis on
specialization." The liberal arts, he argues, should be valued
not because they have "direct and immediate use" but because
they "contribute to a *moral* lesson, the way they change,
shape, and enlarge the vision of those who come in contact
with them. In this way, the liberal arts cultivate thought and
affect the way one understands one's own life and the lives of
others. At the core is the value of wisdom, which is different
than the knowledge derived from instrumental or empirical
studies." For Wagner, a university education that seeks social
"relevance," emphasizes training, or promotes narrow, specialized study undermines the central purposes of higher learning. Specialization in the liberal arts is worthwhile, he notes,

only if it returns the researcher to the fundamental questions of "Who am I? Who are we ... What is right, What is good." Otherwise, it deepens the problem of academic fragmentation and helps destroy the possibility of intellectual community.[11]

Daniel Little disagrees. He believes that what Wagner offers as the core purpose of the liberal arts – the cultivation of values that lead to a humane life – is part of, but not the singular objective of, scholarly life. He argues that the search for "knowledge" – a mission that has "intrinsic value" – is the fundamental goal of liberal education and that specialized study *can* play an important role in this activity. Philosophers, for example, whose knowledge of Wittgenstein is limited to "a series of aphorisms" have merely scratched the surface of the subject, which can be productively penetrated only through in-depth study. Notwithstanding its high ideals, general education can lead less to informed knowledge and understanding than to dilettantism.[12] Indeed, critics challenged the pretensions of Hutchins's "Great Books" approach precisely on these grounds.[13]

In my own field of history, specialization is unavoidable. It takes perhaps five years to complete a project that looks, to all the world, like an exceedingly narrow subject. But how can one not explore the available sources on such questions as the origins of Confederation, living conditions in the Depression, or women's contributions to World War II? In fact, historians frequently lament the lack of time or resources to examine all of the accessible materials on their special subjects. One could choose to write only general surveys, and there certainly is a place for such books in the undergraduate curriculum. But such publications either build on the work of specialist researchers or, in the absence of it, are based on untested generalizations. Furthermore, by exposing students to differing interpretations of similar events by specialist scholars – in history as well as in other disciplines – professors contribute, potentially, to reasoned inquiry and critical thinking in the classroom.

Thus, intensive study of specialized themes has an important place in liberal education, particularly in a world of information glut, where no one can any longer expect to know all that is worth knowing. The university is the ideal, if not the only, institution in society equipped to guide students intelligently through the masses of data, scholarship, opinion, and propaganda that envelop them and now flow ceaselessly from traditional and electronic sources. Intensively probing a single subject or question offers valuable, and applicable, lessons on how to endure and thrive in the "information society."

Still, Wagner and his fellow generalists have an important point. Specialization can be taken to extremes. In universities with few compulsory courses, students could focus on a single subject for their entire academic careers. (Professors generally avoid this by teaching in subjects beyond their research specialization.) If one goal of liberal education is to encourage students to think contextually and to be aware of connections among subjects and disciplines, then exclusive focus on one issue is scarcely advisable.

Most universities employ some form of "breadth requirement" to discourage overspecialization. Students are usually expected to take one-half to two-thirds of their courses in their "major" subject, and the rest from other disciplines. Many institutions require undergraduate exposure to both humanities and social science courses; others go further and compel all arts students to take a course in the physical or natural sciences. Similarly, students in the sciences and the applied fields are generally expected to take at least one course in the arts.

Despite such initiatives, academic cold wars between generalists and specialists, between proponents of the arts and those of the sciences, and between humanists and advocates of applied professionalism still fester. The way forward, I would argue, is a recognition of the principle that both intellectual breadth and specialization are valuable, and together have an essential place in liberal education. Arts students ought to have some basic knowledge of scientific principles and practices, though instructors should teach these subjects creatively and in a way that recognizes the non-specialist nature of their classes. If my own experience many years ago as a first-year student is still typical, compulsory science courses are taught grudgingly and with exceeding dullness by scientists to resentful arts students who make little effort to penetrate the unfamiliar discourse of the astronomer or biologist. A problems-based or issue-oriented course – on the environment or population growth, for example – that probes the scientific dimensions of pertinent social concerns could effectively complement the student's arts studies.[14] Conversely, science students enrolled in the dreaded arts class should be encouraged to explore the social and cultural dimensions of scientific inquiry. Effectively engaged, students might well enjoy rather than merely enduring such courses.

One promising initiative has come from the Canadian Academy for Engineering, which published a report in 1999 that recommended a "broadening of engineering education." It called for curricular revisions in engineering programs that would "ensure the breadth of learning, beyond the technical aspects of the specialist engineering discipline." As the report explained, "Society requires that engineering graduates ... be knowledgeable about the society in which they live and work that they be sensitive to the economic, social, political environmental, cultural and ethical dimensions of their work." Merely obliging engineering students to take the occasional arts courses taught by part-time faculty was a "short-term measure at best," according to the report, which advised that "permanent faculty" should commit themselves to providing a "modern liberal education" to their own students and should "help in improving the technological literacy of all university students as well as the general public."[15] Thus, arts students should have a greater familiarity with science and technology, and those in the applied fields should know more about the social implications of their professional work.

Similar views were expressed in a 1991 report by the Association of American Colleges, which critically reviewed twelve arts and science disciplines and argued that the technical instruction provided in fields such as mathematics, physics, biology, and psychology would be enriched by liberal education. For example:

Mathematics courses have been taught as purely utilitarian courses in techniques, theories and applications. Most courses pay no more than superficial attention to the historical, cultural, or contemporary context in which mathematics is practiced. Today, however, as mathematical models are used increasingly for policy and operation purposes of immense consequence, it is vitally important the students learn to think through these issues even as they learn the details of mathematics itself. Examples abound of mathematical activity that leads directly to decisions of great human import. Mathematical models of global warming, computer-controlled trading of stocks, and epidemiological studies of AIDS illustrate how mathematics really matters in important decisions affecting daily life.[16]

Innovations in the medical education field well illustrate the ways in which liberal studies, academic science, and clinical training can be effectively combined to improve the quality of higher learning and medical practice. Traditionally, medical students have been steeped in a narrow, scientific educational process that concentrates on the "disease and not the patient." Complaints in the 1930s that "the specialist looks too frequently upon the problem of the patient solely from the aspect of his specialty, rather than from the needs of the patient as a whole"[17] were echoed in 1999 by a professor of clinical surgery at Yale, who claimed that faculty members had been rewarded more for specialized research than "for teaching well, or for caring for (or even about) patients."[18]

New initiatives in medical education, however, focus on issues central to the social sciences. Perhaps the most innovative such program is that of the internationally renown McMaster Medical School in Hamilton, Ontario. Opened in 1966, the school employed admission procedures and pedagogy that departed dramatically from the practices of traditional medical schools. While the latter have compelled applicants to have a strong background in the biological sciences and to excel in the medical college admission test, McMaster has not required these, nor has it privileged candidates with high grades. Instead, "students who have previously majored in the humanities and social sciences," those with varied experiences and interests, and those committed to group-based, problem-solving learning strategies are more likely to be admitted. In addition, recruitment committees – which include current medical students – engage short-listed applicants in personal interviews (unlike most medical schools).

Throughout the medical training program, McMaster students meet in small groups led by a faculty tutor. "Various aspects of a health problem – ranging from the basic science concepts needed to understand the patho-physiology, through the impact on the patient and the family – are identified by group members who seek out the appropriate learning resources in order to acquire the knowledge with which to manage the problem. The basic and clinical sciences are presented in an integrative manner, rather than individually. The learning approach emphasizes the student as an active learner and places more responsibility for their education on students. Lectures, called large-group resource sessions, are few and are optional for the student. About 20 per cent of the program is devoted to student-selected electives." The program encourages and seeks to improve upon the "life-long learning habits of physicians."[19] Surveyed regularly, McMaster students have consistently praised this active form of instruction, as have external assessors: "The school has achieved most of its goals: more and better community oriented doctors, a more enjoyable curriculum and one which offered choice, early clinical contact and a humanistic approach to its students."[20]

Another medical school initiative flowed from a resolution at the World Summit on Medical Education in 1993, which called upon medical education to become more "community oriented," to focus students' attention on "real world settings," and to encourage them to "respond to the needs of society."[21] This led to a new course, now compulsory for University of Toronto medical students, called "Health, Illness and the Community." The course requires students in first and second year to spend one half-day per week working in placements that involve some three hundred community agencies and to explore the issues arising from their experiences. Students first observe patients in their residences in order to understand better how "people cope with illness and disability in the home environment." They then spend time at a public health unit, where they are exposed to such issues as "domestic violence, sexually transmitted diseases and smoking cessation." This is followed by a section in the course on "health determinants and health promotion strategies" and includes two agency placements that address these themes. In their second year, students focus on the "interconnection between a health problem and a social issue." Coordination between community agencies and teaching hospitals enable students to grapple directly with the medical and social elements of the issues they are investigating. Throughout the two-year course, students are exposed to a variety of readings from social science fields.

The program has been assessed positively by students, patients, and agencies. Students especially appreciate the field placements, though as Wasylenki, Cohen, and McRobb note, "the course is weaker on the theoretical side, because an integrating conceptual model has not yet been developed."[22] Improving the course thus requires a more effective melding of the academic and hands-on approaches. Even in its early phase, the course has demonstrated the potential value of a training program that combines social and medical science, and the virtue of grappling with health problems within a social context. Whether it will actually produce physicians who employ more holistic, community-based forms of medical practice remains to be seen. But in challenging traditional disciplinary boundaries between the applied sciences and social sciences, it is a promising initiative.

One further curricular trend ought to be noted. Signifying other social and cultural changes, liberal education has become increasingly multidisciplinary and interdisciplinary. In the past generation, programs in such fields as communications studies, health and society, urban studies, environmental studies, industrial relations, labour studies, and practical ethics have been introduced at numerous universities. These subjects also signify the erosion of disciplinary borders and the creation of new curricular syntheses. Scholars in these fields seek to bring academic conceptions to bear on current social problems, frequently providing forums for critical reflection and policy development.

Thus, while a liberal education can no longer pretend to cover every field of knowledge, it can help students navigate their way through oceans of good and bad information and can help them trace the links between various and, at first glance, unrelated fields of study. It can simultaneously encourage the student to appreciate the ways in which Plato, Shakespeare, and also contemporary clinical psychologists, have sought to understand human motivation and behaviour. Most importantly, through a sensible combination of academic breadth and specialized study, it can perhaps remind students and society at large of the intrinsic value of continual learning.

Diversity and Tolerance

Universities serve broader student constituencies than they did through much of the twentieth century. Women, once a mere token presence on campus, now constitute the majority of undergraduates in Canada and the United States. Those from religious and racial minority groups, once virtually excluded by discriminatory admission policies, are a visible presence, especially at universities in large urban centres with culturally diverse populations. Students from wealthier families are still more likely to attend university than the poor, though even with respect to social class there has been some degree of democratization. A 1994 survey of first-year students in seven universities across Canada found that 48 per cent came from families with average incomes under $49,000. The median family income in Canada in 1994 was $48,091.[23]

Curriculum development, as we have seen, responds to a variety of intellectual currents and social forces. One is the identity of those who teach and study in universities. In an era when English Canadian students and their professors typically came from white, Anglo-Celtic, Protestant backgrounds, the curriculum reflected their heritage, interests, and values. History and politics courses focused on the evolution of Canada within the British Empire. English literature was literally just that: the (male) novelists, poets, and critics of England, and only occasionally of the United States or English Canada.

American liberal education similarly promoted national (and nationalist) interests that reflected the experiences and beliefs of the society's dominant cultural groups and elites.[24]

The changing nature of the student and faculty constituencies was bound to affect the curriculum. In particular, courses on the experiences of women and of non-dominant groups are far more common than in the past. As noted in chapter 1, the inclusion of such curricula has sparked heated debates among liberal arts educators about the nature of "essential" knowledge – a debate that reflects contemporary concerns about ethnic, racial, and gender relations in the broader community. Unlike other institutions that have sometimes suppressed or avoided such discussions, universities – admittedly, often under duress – have engaged these issues.

It is time, in my view, for the university to move beyond such debates. As a historian of education, I can no longer conceive of writing the history of schooling without reference to the experience of female teachers and students. Similarly, many historians and sociologists now appreciate the interest that students from minority groups or immigrant communities have in exploring their own roots, and university curricula increasingly reflect those concerns (though, certainly, this is not all that such students should study). Course work on Native communities, on life in developing countries, and on lesbian and gay issues also signifies the university's efforts to address intellectually the experiences of traditionally ignored or marginalized groups.

These initiatives to promote curricular diversity should enrich academic life, not diminish it, and I find the Bloom-like complaint that feminism and multiculturalism have contributed to such alleged tragedies as the "killing" of Canadian history[25] to be unpersuasive. Those who believe that the primary purpose of history is to contribute to the traditional goal of nation building are entitled to explore the past with that mission in mind. But other researchers have different goals and perspectives, for which they should not be denounced – except if their scholarship is demonstrably deficient. Surely, the health of the liberal arts, let alone the principle of academic freedom, requires scholars to respect the academic choices, even if they dispute the methodologies or research findings of their colleagues.

This applies, too, to the proponents of the new curricula. Social historians, for example, should neither ignore nor disparage the study of political history, especially in a country that was built and will endure only through the process of political negotiation; it is myopic to dismiss the study of politicians' actions as the mere study of "elites." Ideally, academics with different perspectives would meld the complementary aspects of their scholarship to create new syntheses, and live respectfully with the irreconcilable elements. Those postmodernists who doubt that truth is discoverable should at least abide with the efforts of colleagues who believe otherwise. I also think that liberal education is in jeopardy if we accept the argument of some that one cannot teach and write outside of own's own cultural experience. By this logic, non-aboriginals would avoid research of First Nations societies, and perhaps only women would pay attention to women's lives. Among other casualties of this approach would be the discipline of history itself, for how could any of us pretend to understand earlier societies in which we did not live? Liberal education should seek to liberate the literary imagination, not confine it. There is no reasonable alternative to civil discourse and tolerance of diverse perspectives in the contemporary university, and these practices ought now to be included as fundamental components of liberal education.

Within this framework, are there any legitimate restrictions on intellectual work, or are academics free to employ any and all research and teaching methods? Ethical concerns impose certain limits. Researchers in the sciences and social sciences are generally required by funding agencies to ensure that the privacy and dignity of human subjects are protected and respected. Participation by individuals in research projects must be voluntary, not coerced or exploitive, and the subjects' identities must be undetectable. Similar standards should apply to students writing term essays. For example, individuals interviewed in the course of a research project cannot be named without their written permission.

Are there any limits on how controversial a professor can be in the classroom? In recent years, incidents have erupted in which students have accused professors, by virtue of what they have said or written, of being "racist" or "sexist," and some of these faculty have subsequently faced professional sanctions. As I have argued, liberal education must include, fundamentally, a respect for the principles of diversity and tolerance, and these altercations have arisen from debates about how the "inclusive" university ought to function. In their teaching or grading practices, faculty who humiliate students or discriminate against them on the basis of their gender, race, religion, ethnicity, or sexual orientation violate basic tenets of liberal education and, in all likelihood, are engaging in professional misconduct. The tolerant and inclusive university ought to prohibit such practices and effectively confront them if they do occur.

Many controversial cases, however, are less clear cut than the overt act of racism or sexism. An especially difficult one involved Philippe Rushton, a psychology professor at the University of Western Ontario, who assembled social science research data (first published in 1989) that demonstrated, in his view, the role of racial origin in the ordering of human intelligence. He contended that "Mongoloids" have higher average intelligence levels than "Caucasoids," who in turn rank higher than "Negroids." As John Fekete noted, Rushton, a prolific scholar, "did not claim that these hypotheses can predict individual variation ... or that they can serve as the basis for any social, legal, or political policies that would single out members of a racial group for discriminatory treatment."[26] Nor was there evidence that the professor behaved in racist ways in the university's classroom or corridors. Complaints about the unsavouriness of Rushton's research led the premier of Ontario to call for his firing. Furthermore, the Ontario Provincial Police investigated whether he had violated Canadian law by promoting racial hatred, though no charges were laid. Ultimately, academic freedom provisions were invoked to protect Rushton's position at the university.

The notion of liberal education that I am articulating in this chapter would support this outcome. It is difficult to conceive how the autonomy of scholars and students, to say nothing of their right to think and write critically, could be respected if offensive scholarship were prohibited and petulant scholars censured. By these criteria, the censorship net could catch – as it did in the past – academic radicals of the political left, who were kept out of, harassed, or hounded from the university.[27] The principles of civility, diversity and tolerance require the university to embrace a variety of academic cultures as well as different human constituencies.

But no reasonable notion of liberal education, or professional responsibility, obligates – or permits – universities to countenance acts of discrimination and racial or sexual harassment by faculty or students. Nor does the university condone academic fraud. Just as students can be penalized for plagiarism, so too professors who invent data or are proven to be professionally incompetent should be declared unfit. If "offensive" (or any other) research is based on fraudulent scholarship, the researcher ought to be admonished and probably dismissed. Short of such demonstrations of professional incompetence or misconduct, controversial teachers and researchers ought to be protected by regulations governing academic freedom. Liberal education in the contemporary era requires it.

Community Participation

Universities have long been burdened by their image as "ivory towers," occupied by monklike scholars who are isolated from and unwilling to communicate with the world beyond their cloistered gates. While the addled brilliant professor can still be found wandering the halls (or hiding in his office), the ivory tower is by now a mere caricature of the university. Arguably, higher education has never, even in the Middle Ages, been untouched by and unengaged with the external community.

Today, politicians, corporations, taxpayers, and tuition-paying families make enormous demands on postsecondary education in exchange for their patronage of the institutions. University presidents spend increasing amounts of time lobbying potential sponsors for resources and mounting expensive public relations campaigns to promote the accomplishments of their teachers and students. Indeed, in the competitive, unforgiving educational marketplace, universities that ignore the surrounding community do so at their peril.

Not all of the external pressures exerted on the university are beneficial (as we shall see in chapter 4), but at its best, scholarly life can benefit from and contribute to a healthy community, and liberal education has a vital role to play in such interaction. Socrates recognized this principle. In historian Martha Nussbaum's words, he contended that argument "is essential to a strong democracy and to any lasting pursuit of justice." Nussbaum maintained: "In order to foster a democracy that is reflective and deliberative, rather than simply a marketplace of competing interest groups, democracy that genuinely takes thought for the common good, we must produce citizens who have the Socratic capacity to reason about their beliefs ... This failure to think critically produces a democracy in which people talk at one another but never have a genuine dialogue. In such an atmosphere bad arguments pass for good arguments, and prejudice can all too easily masquerade as reason."[28]

Politicians frequently perpetuate this problem, attempting to say as little of substance as possible and using visual media as their instruments, thus "communicating" on the basis of image, personality, and clichés. According to Adrienne Bond, "When a new secretary of state makes a policy statement on human rights, 'There will be no de-emphasis but a change in priority,' we [should] see past the vigor and self-confidence and know that he is talking nonsense, that he knows he is talking nonsense, and that he assumes that we will not know the difference. These are important things for us to know."[29] Courses in media literacy, political philosophy, language study, or ethics, if taught and studied effectively, should help improve the quality of the student's participation in social and political affairs – or at least should make him or her a more discerning voter.

A study by the American Institute for Higher Education Policy contends that the prospects for "social cohesion" and "appreciation of diversity" rise with higher levels of education. Higher education generates "social connectedness" and "an appreciation for a diverse society ... Those with more than a high school education have significantly more trust in social institutions and participate in civic and community groups at much higher rates than others."[30]

Applied subjects in fields such as business require more than accounting and marketing courses if graduates are to bring "added value" to the world of commerce. A business ethics teacher argues that business teaching that ignores the principle that "all knowledge is self-knowledge" is constraining and potentially harmful. As public enterprises become increasingly privatized, he says, business executives have a larger role than ever as "social leaders." They should be "introspective" and more fully aware of the social impact of their boardroom decisions. Ethical issues from "whistle blowing" to "product safety" compel business people to "wrestle with their own standards of right and wrong, their self conceptions and character"[31] – again, issues central to liberal education. Indeed, a biology professor argues that the liberal arts ought to be an integral part of professional and technical courses: "A university graduate needs to be aware of the ethical, social and cultural context of her work to avoid, at the very least, causing potential harm. An engineer who can design a cost-effective dam that can hold a mighty river, yet is unaware of the potential social and environmental consequences of building it, is dangerous."[32] In response to recent corporate scandals, product recalls, and public (including shareholder) concerns about investment practices, particularly in developing countries, a number of corporations, such as Canadian Occidental Petroleum Ltd., have introduced ethics training programs that "encompass rules from business conduct to employee and human rights as well as the environment,"[33] concerns central to the humanities and social sciences.

That universities play a greater role than ever in the educational lives of Canadians also underlines their social importance. It is still the case that students from affluent families or families where parents have a postsecondary education are more likely than others to attend university. However, between 1982 and 1993 the participation rate in university of those in the population aged eighteen to twenty-four rose from 12 to 20 per cent.[34] This expansion was accounted for largely by the growing participation of women in higher education. Between 1975 and 1995 the number of men in universities increased by 25 per cent and that of women by 107 per cent; and the latter, as noted earlier, are now the majority of undergraduate students in Canada. More than men, they choose to study in the liberal arts.[35] De-emphasizing these subjects will thus target areas in which women have the greatest involvement, possibly reversing the social progress of recent years. The university's part in promoting gender equality in society should not be overlooked, and the liberal arts have been and continue to be a clear catalyst in this process.

Similarly, universities have played a central role in the world of "adult learning," in which the opportunity for advanced education is available to traditionally excluded groups. This movement has its roots in the history of adult education initiatives taken in Britain, the United States, and Canada. A host of "self-improvement" societies in eighteenth- and nineteenth-century America reflected "the pursuit of knowledge under difficulties" by ordinary citizens.[36] Mechanics' institutes, begun in Britain in the 1820s, spread to North America and provided a forum for literate artisans and tradesmen to discuss philosophical and social issues and laid the foundation for the creation of public libraries. Workers' educational associations formed in the early twentieth century also stressed the value of liberal education. And in all three countries, adult education associations, which sought to improve society by encouraging citizens to extend – or begin – their pursuit of knowledge, were especially active between the two world wars.[37] Perhaps the most compelling adult education initiative in Canada was the postwar veterans' educational program, begun in 1943, which provided free tuition and living allowances to some 40,000 individuals who chose to resume or begin their university studies at the end of their military service.[38]

Broad participation in adult learning continues today. In 1997, some six million (or 28 per cent of) adults in Canada partook in adult education and training activities. While most such schooling was job-related, a significant minority of Canadians participated for reasons of personal interest. It is notable that those with the highest levels of education were the most inclined to pursue adult learning, suggesting that the opportunity to pursue schooling generates even higher demand for additional education.[39]

Schuller and Bostyn argue that the combination of "increased longevity and early retirement" will generate more interest still in purposeful and fulfilling leisure activities among an aging population, especially in adult education, from which both individuals and society should derive benefit. Students surveyed at Wandsworth College, a large adult education institute in London, England, ranked the benefits of their schooling in the following way: "Keeping my mind active, 72 per cent; developing knowledge of a subject, 68 per cent; making new friends, 57 per cent, developing a practical skill, 42 per cent, gaining more confidence, 40 per cent."[40] Continual learning that combines intellectual, social, and applied elements thus appears to find resonance among these adult learners.

An intriguing example of the possibilities of adult education is the program inaugurated by American historian Earl Shorris, who began a humanities course for poor youth in a deprived New York community and later did so in several other cities, including Vancouver. In a series of academically demanding courses, students studied ancient philosophy, poetry, art history, mathematical logic, or American history. Through the auspices of the Roberto Clemente Center, donors and volunteers provided students with the bus fare and a sandwich, as well as daycare for their children. Sixteen of the thirty students who enrolled in the first year of the program graduated from it, and ten of those later went to a four-year college or nursing school; the remainder were in community college or employed full-time.[41]

The strength of such a program appeared to lie in the instructors' willingness to solicit and take seriously students' ideas and to teach without condescension. The students discussed conceptions of justice and freedom and participated in problem solving, drawing frequently for illustrations on their own troubled lives. For the first time they experienced, and apparently appreciated, the rewards of a humanities education. The program continues to expand.

Thus, the elitism with which liberal education has been traditionally associated is now challenged by such innovations and by historically high participation rates in higher education. More than ever, our society has the opportunity to provide the stimulation that liberal education offers to sizable portions of the community, an opportunity that it would be foolish to limit or forgo.

Effective Communication

As we have seen, liberal education has always emphasized students' abilities to express themselves successfully. Elegant speaking or writing are intrinsically rewarding, but they serve a broader purpose as well. They are the means by which thought and ideas are communicated to others and through which intelligent dialogue is sustained. Even while the goals of liberal education changed throughout history, this objective remained constant. In Ancient Greece and Rome, orators used the town square to articulate their views on law and justice. Medieval scholars wrote and lectured on the principles and nuances of Christian theology. Eventually, the successful oral defence of a dissertation became the student's crowning academic achievement, witnessed by his peers, his masters, and frequently the public.

With the establishment of the first publishing houses in sixteenth-century Europe, written communication became more common and its forms more varied, though most people in Europe and North America were unable to read or write until well into the nineteenth century. Children learned by observation and emulation, and one could become a skilled farmer or craftsman without being "literate" in the contemporary sense. The spread of public schooling, prompted by steady urbaniza- tion, the more specialized needs of industry and economic life, and the desire by ordinary citizens for the knowledge and sta- tus that literacy provided, generated greater demand for pub- lished work. By the mid-twentieth century, the modern uni- versity was a major centre (though not necessarily the only place) in which advanced writing was taught and practised. Liberal educators now expected students to write analytical essays, research reports, fiction, and poetry. For professors, scholarly publication became the chief currency of academic life, the accrual of which shaped the course of one's career.

By the late twentieth century, liberal educators still valued the oral tradition and paid some deference to the traditional ideal of developing the student's "character," but these goals were no longer systematically pursued. Students were still required to learn by *listening* to lectures, and they were rewarded in seminars for being thoughtful and articulate, but mainly they were expected to write successful papers and examinations in a *text*-based educational system. The accu- mulation of knowledge and the ability to penetrate some of its mysteries is, in the contemporary university, the presumed route to intellectual liberation.

Professors in the arts thus encourage students to translate their thoughts into writing and to express them coherently and eloquently, both because this is an intellectually fulfilling exer- cise and because it has endless value in the world beyond the university. Reading perceptively, thinking creatively, and writ- ing clearly enable individuals to define their values better and to find their authentic voices. As we shall note in the next chapter, the practical uses of these skills are enormous.

Indeed, effective communication is essential in the sciences as well as the arts. The (Canadian-born) Harvard scientist and

Nobel laureate David Hubel advises students that their chief mission in university should be to "learn to write English really well." For their work to be appreciated by the non-specialist community, and to stimulate informed discussion about the important social implications of their research, scientists should attempt to impart their knowledge lucidly to broad audiences. According to University of Toronto chemist John Polanyi, another Nobel Prize winner, science students would benefit especially from a liberal arts education that teaches them how to trace patterns in human thought, behaviour, and experience: "In science we look for those patterns not in the language of poetry but in such languages as numbers and algebra."[42] Explaining this process in comprehensible language, as the biologist Stephen Jay Gould and geneticist David Suzuki have done so skilfully, contributes intellectually, politically, *and* scientifically to the health of the community.

This discussion, of course, reflects an idealized view of liberal learning, and intellectual life itself, in the university, but in this chapter our sights have been set purposely high. Before confronting the obstacles that stand in the way of these goals, we must have identifiable and defensible objectives. The impediments to achieving and sustaining them are indeed real. As I argue in the remainder of this book, they come in the form of utilitarian pressures that narrow the university's vision and threaten to marginalize scholarly endeavour. They arise from ill-conceived policies supported and forced upon universities by businesses and government. They emerge, too, from popular culture, in which text-based notions of literacy have been challenged by the video, electronic, and digital revolutions. Is it possible that students neither share nor relate to their professors' academic ideals? All of this could be grounds for despair or the basis for renewed critical and creative thinking.

In this chapter, I have posited a particular definition of liberal education, fully aware that other interpretations exist and have merit. But my reading of many of them is that they are overly general or rooted in nostalgia. I believe that we should draw inspiration from and retain the workable ideas of ancient scholars, but neither liberal education nor higher education more broadly can merely reiterate the past. Higher learning is affected though not necessarily deluged by cultural, intellectual, political, and economic changes. The challenge is to preserve the university's integrity in the face of such pressures. Using the techniques of liberal learning itself, I have attempted to present a reasoned defence of liberal education. The dialogue will continue only if liberal education itself is respected and sustained.

3

Occupations, Incomes, and the Economy

This book argues that liberal education is its own justification. Immersing oneself in the world of ideas and navigating through countervailing intellectual currents is challenging and intrinsically rewarding. The discoveries one makes on such a voyage are often as stirring and stimulating as the ultimate destination itself.

Yet for a variety of reasons, in the world of education, the ends often trump the means. Consumed by the values of the marketplace, governments, employers, the media, parents, and students habitually assess schooling not for what it is but for what it can purchase. The politician who speaks of society's educational "investment" is not merely proffering a metaphor. He or she wants to know how schooling will contribute to economic growth. Will it help fill labour shortages or compound the problem of unemployment by turning out people with qualifications and skills which the market supposedly no longer prizes? Will students "profit" from their investments in higher education by securing lucrative employment upon graduation, and will they in turn contribute further to economic life by paying bountiful taxes and generating jobs for others? Will higher education help make Canada more competitive in the ubiquitous global economy?

These are unquestionably important matters, but in such calculations liberal education is frequently assumed to fare poorly. As the premier of Ontario sarcastically contended, "We seem to be graduating more people who are great thinkers, but they know nothing about math or science or engineering or the skill sets that are needed."[1] What, after all, could philosophers or English majors contribute to the needs of the banking or information technology industries?

The answer to such a question is "quite a lot," and this chapter attempts to explain what economic benefits liberal education offers both to the individual and to society at large. For the moment, at least, this book enters into the "education-as-investment" discourse, partly in an effort to refute the Ontario premier's assertion and partly to respond to the concerns of others who have legitimate questions about the economic value of higher learning. But I undertake this task cautiously. This chapter is not an argument for assessing liberal education's value exclusively or even primarily in economic terms. Yet even if utilitarian preoccupations are given their due, the social sciences and humanities, contrary to popular belief, prove their worth. Society would be the poorer culturally and economically in their absence.

In Diane Francis's view, supporters of liberal education should go back to school. The former editor of Canada's *Financial Post* posed and answered this question: "Does Canada need more sociology and psychology majors? Does it need more MBAS and English literature graduates? Or do we need more bricklayers, computer technologists and others with practical skills in food, health or financial services ... Huge proportions of university graduates with degrees are under- or unemployed because they find themselves trained for nothing."[2]

Many Canadians would appear to agree. In one opinion poll, 52 per cent of respondents would have encouraged young people to attend a community college in order to obtain a "skill" or "trade," while just 36 per cent would have advised them to get a "general" university education. (The question assumed that these goals could not be pursued simultaneously.)[3] Another survey of Ontario residents found 35 per cent believing that "the most valuable type of education to have in the work force 10 years from now" would be a college diploma in a technical occupation, with only 3 per cent favouring a university degree in the arts. More respondents (13 per cent) believed that a high school diploma and "lots of on-the-job training" would serve one better in the economy of the future than a university arts degree would.[4]

By linking college and technical training with "skills" and "occupations," the questions in these surveys, let alone the answers, reinforced the common view that a "general" university education serves a functionally questionable purpose. Technical training is assumed to be practical; higher learning, superfluous. The former is supposedly tied to the "real" world and earns the student measurable material rewards; the latter floats aimlessly and unprofitably in the abstract world of ideas. As we shall see, those who hold such views – whether premiers, journalists, or ordinary citizens – couldn't be more wrong.

There is no shortage of prominent business commentators who favour a university system driven predominantly by "market forces" and corporate demand. The Toronto Board of Trade, for example, issued a statement in 1998 calling for the deregulation of tuition fees, greater institutional specialization and rationalization of programs, and private universities "both for-profit and non-profit."[5] P.C. Godsoe, the CEO of Scotiabank, urged business to participate more than ever in university curricular development, "making sure that programs are aimed at real needs, real skills and real benefits to the student and to our community." Today's "global competition and technological revolution" demand no less from universities, he stated.[6]

Such corporate prescriptions have ominous implications for liberal education, whose relevance and utility are so frequently doubted; as we shall see in the next chapter, government policy has increasingly been swayed by this world view. Partly in response to the pervasiveness of such thinking, an impressive group of successful business leaders (many with arts degrees) has spoken out in support of university teaching in the humanities and social sciences. Most notably, chief executive officers from thirty corporations, including Bell Canada, IBM, Xerox of Canada, Compaq Canada, and many others from the information and high-technology sectors, issued a statement in the spring of 2000 enthusiastically endorsing the liberal arts. "A liberal arts and science education," they claimed, "nurtures skills and talents increasingly valued by modern corporations. Our companies function in a state of constant flux. To prosper we need creative thinkers at all levels of the enterprise who are comfortable dealing with decisions in the bigger context. They must be able to communicate – to reason, create, write and speak – for shared purposes: for hiring, training, managing, marketing, and policymaking. In short, they provide leadership."[7]

Testimony from individual business executives, schooled in the arts, reinforces this view. Gordon Cheesborough, chief executive officer of Altamira Financial Services Ltd, a leading mutual funds company, majored in philosophy. In his view, "an arts education broadens your horizons. Technology is important, but the best ideas may not come from people with a technological background." He seeks potential employees with a "heightened sense of curiosity ... Well-read people with broad interests, these are our problem solvers." Of course specialized industry-specific proficiency is necessary, but in his experience new employees with university degrees "pick up technical skills on the job."[8] Theresa Carbonneau, president and chief executive officer of Fsona Corp., a wireless networking startup company, holds a master's degree in sociology. Like numerous other executives, she contends that contemporary companies require employees who can talk to customers in language they can understand, a skill likely to be cultivated in arts programs. Jeffrey Kearney, who works with a business that develops computer games, notes that his industry is "grappling with issues of violence and sexism," questions which computer programming graduates have generally not confronted. Hillary Horlock, a co-founder of IdeaPark Communications Inc. in Vancouver, graduated in English and history, which she credits with providing her with "the ability to think and to be totally unfettered in the search for answers."[9]

Business students themselves, trained exclusively in operational techniques, will in all likelihood prove less successful than the commerce graduates who have some understanding of social psychology, community dynamics, or cultural life in the countries in which companies invest – knowledge gained through liberal arts education. As the American scholar Michael Useem points out, business practitioners who understand foreign languages and a community's environmental concerns can help smooth a company's path into foreign markets.[10] The deputy minister of Western Economic Development for the federal government, Oryssia Lennie, anticipates a growth of the Canadian public sector, which requires "people who can think, who are flexible ... who can thrive in a complex and challenging environment." There is a "tremendous need for arts graduates," she told participants at the 2000 Congress of the Social Sciences and Humanities. "I don't think you have any idea of just how critical your skills are."[11] Reinforcing this point, John Cleghorn, chairman of the Royal Bank of Canada, claimed that 50 to 60 per cent of the people the bank hired were arts and science graduates. "What a liberal arts education gives somebody," he asserted, "is a great grounding for communication skills; it broadens your interpersonal skills and these are the kinds of people we look for."[12] For all of these commentators, the social sciences and humanities are a vital, not an unprofitable, investment for the individual, the corporation, and the community.

Such concerns may well explain why chief executive officers in a major American survey on the benefits of a college education had a broader perspective on the value of higher learning than parents and college-bound students did. The latter two groups focused mostly on the short-term outcome of "getting a job," while the former considered, far more frequently, the long-term benefits of higher education. As the author noted, employers in the survey were presumably no less practically minded than parents and students. "But to them practicality means the ability of higher education to impact general skills that give people the flexibility and capacity to keep learning what today's high-tech businesses require ... They insist that a college education produce people of strong character with generalized intellectual and social skills and a capacity for learning." The particular facilities that human resource managers valued were threefold: cognitive (problem-solving, critical thinking, and learning to learn), presentational (oral and written communication skills), and social (working cooperatively in a variety of settings).[13]

An earlier American study of corporate recruitment practices found a strong interest in graduates who had "a combination of the liberal and practical skills."[14] Indeed, business leaders surveyed by the American Council on Education felt that universities and colleges were inadequately equipping graduates with such necessary on-the-job requirements as "communication skills, the ability to work in teams, flexibility, the ability to accept ambiguity comfortably, the ability to work with people from diverse backgrounds, understanding of globalization and its implications, and adequate ethics training" – all skills that liberal education should be able to foster.[15] The Conference Board of Canada's 2000 list of "employability skills" highlighted similar aptitudes that broadly educated graduates could bring to their jobs.[16]

The attitude of company executives to liberal education matters a good deal because it affects recruitment strategies within their organizations. Where the corporate culture favours the hiring of liberal arts graduates, recruitment officers are more inclined to do so. Conversely, company presidents who stress more narrowly focused technical and business qualifications discourage the employment of the more liberally educated. At times, the views of the senior spokespersons and the officials responsible for hiring are in conflict, and the graduate may get a mixed message about the value of his or her liberal education background, something that can confound the job search.[17]

How, indeed, have university graduates from the liberal arts fared in the workforce, particularly in comparison to those from the supposedly more "market-worthy" disciplines? The image of the underemployed graduate with a PHD in literature is by now an iconic symbol of wasted investment in higher learning, for both the student and society. As we shall see, there are such individuals, but they are hardly typical. University graduates are by no means insulated from the adverse effects of economic restructuring and recession, but the advantages of those in fields such as commerce and engineering over those from the social sciences and humanities, particularly in the long term, are at best marginal. These groups together face the burden of hard times and share in the bounty of growing

prosperity. Collectively, whatever the general economic conditions, they have better employment opportunities and higher
incomes than college, technical, vocational, or high school
graduates. Using different data sets and methodologies, several studies published during the 1990s (an exceedingly volatile
economic period) bear out these conclusions, and the following section highlights some of their findings.

The National Graduate Surveys, conducted by Statistics
Canada, has surveyed graduates of Canadian universities for
more than a decade. Its reports on the employment experience
of 1990 graduates were based on responses from more than
30,000 individuals. It found that two years after graduation
(1992), former university students had felt the impact of the
recession of the early 1990s, as their unemployment rate averaged 11 per cent (see table 1).[18] The rate was slightly above
this level for humanities and social science graduates, and
slightly below for engineering (and applied sciences) and commerce (and management and administration) graduates. The
situation improved significantly by 1995. Five years after

Table 1

National graduate survey: Unemployment rate of 1990 university graduates by field of study

	1992	1995
All fields of study	11	6
Agriculture and biological sciences	11	9
Commerce, management, and administration	8	4
Education	8	3
Engineering and applied sciences	11	5
Fine and applied arts	15	12
Health professions	5	3
Mathematics and physical sciences	11	6
Humanities	14	9
Social sciences	12	6

Source: Paju, "The Class of '90 Revisited," 22

graduation, as the recession receded, the class of 1990 had an average unemployment rate of 6 per cent, again slightly higher for those from the humanities and social sciences, and slightly lower for engineering and commerce graduates. Graduates from the health professions and education had the lowest unemployment rates. Clearly, an improving economy in the mid-1990s benefited university graduates as a whole.

As the decade progressed, these patterns continued. Axelrod, Anisef, and Lin examined Canadian census data between 1971 and 1996, dividing university graduates between those who were twenty-five to twenty-nine years old, and those who were over thirty years of age. They found that the employment situation improved significantly for all graduates as they aged. The unemployment rate in 1996 by field of study for the former group was 6.5 per cent for fine arts, 9.4 per cent for humanities, 7.9 per cent for social sciences, 5.9 per cent for commerce, 7.4 per cent for engineering, and 7.7 per cent for math and physical sciences, indicating a marginal advantage for those in business and sciences. For graduates thirty years and up, the unemployment rates were 6.4 per cent for fine arts, 6 per cent for humanities, 4.5 per cent for social sciences, 3.9 per cent for commerce, and 5.2 per cent for engineering. Note that the social sciences unemployment rate was lower than for engineering, a field that is particularly sensitive to abrupt shifts in the economy.[19]

The research of economist Robert C. Allen sustained the case for the economic value of higher education. "The view that most university graduates [in the arts] have particular trouble finding work," he noted, "is contradicted by Census data."[20] Nor was the advantaged position of university graduates – whatever their field of study – merely a result of "credential inflation," in which the highly educated take over low-paying jobs once occupied by the less educated. The job market is not static – new occupations are created even as others disappear. In the 1980s and 1990s, managerial and professional employment grew significantly, and university graduates, far more than other groups, occupied these positions.[21] University graduates in sales and service occupations, another growth sector, earned far higher salaries than individuals with less education, and thus they should not be perceived as having slipped down the occupational ladder. The fact that university graduates, even through a heavy recession, continued to earn more than others meant that the economic value of the degree in the marketplace had not diminished in Canada, and it underlined the contention of the Organization for Economic Co-operation and Development (OECD) that there was a steady and continuing labour market demand for people with higher education.[22]

It is notable that this analysis applied to humanities and social science graduates as fully as it did to those in business, engineering, and applied science. In 1991 the majority of graduates – between 50 and 60 per cent of men and women with bachelor degrees in the arts – were employed in managerial and professional occupations, and these figures rose significantly for those with master's and doctoral degrees.[23] Furthermore, the incomes of those in the humanities and social sciences compared favourably, particularly as the individuals aged, with those in other fields. For women in their fifties who held a bachelor's degree, the average income was $46,000 in 1991. Humanities graduates earned $46,000, social sciences graduates $47,000, commerce graduates $48,000, and physical sciences and mathematics graduates $39,000. Income gaps by field of study were greater for women in their twenties, which demonstrated that as graduates got older, those in the humanities and social sciences increased their earnings more rapidly than those from other fields.

Income differences by field of study for men in their fifties were greater than for women. But the differences did not especially favour applied science and commerce graduates over those from the social sciences and humanities. Engineers, who were at the top of the income scale, earned $79,000 (1995 dollars), social science graduates $78,000, mathematics and physical science graduates $70,000, and commerce graduates $69,000. Those in education earned $56,000, those in humanities and fine arts $57,000, those in agriculture and biology $60,000, and those in other health fields $54,000. Like the women, men with humanities and social science degrees witnessed a more rapid growth of their incomes as they got older than those in other fields did. As Allen explained, those in the liberal arts tend not to move immediately into long-term occupational positions (compared with those trained in specific professions) because it takes time for them to "construct their own career ladders." This, he says, "means that the rewards are delayed, so earnings increase steeply with age and experience."[24] In any event, the employment and income experiences of university graduates were significantly better, both in the short term and long term, than those without university education.

Provincial surveys in Alberta and Ontario underlined these conclusions, though they reported only on shorter-term employment outcomes. The Alberta Graduate Survey traced the employment experiences of students who graduated in 1994 and were in the labour market in 1997. In the midst of a booming provincial economy, only 3.5 per cent of this group was unemployed, compared with an overall provincial unemployment rate of 6 per cent and a national unemployment rate of 9 per cent. Those in the arts and sciences had unemployment rates somewhat above the 3.5 per cent rate (4.4 per cent for engineering, 4.7 per cent for social science, and 8.3 per cent for biological science graduates). Graduates in certain professional areas fared better: from medicine there was zero per cent unemployment rate and from law only 0.9 per cent, while the unemployment rate from education was 2.6 per cent.

Arts graduates earned lower salaries than those in health care, the professions and applied science and were less likely to be in jobs that "fitted" their educational backgrounds. Did this indicate that the humanities and social sciences served graduates poorly in the labour market? In some cases, possibly. (I discuss the issue of underemployment in more detail below.) But Krahn and Lowe argued that the reverse may well have been the case: the fact that such graduates found work in a variety of occupations indicated that "these general arts or science programs help prepare individuals for a wide range of rewarding careers" and that they "were in jobs that took advantage of the general skills and abilities acquired in [their academic] program[s]."[25]

Finally, a survey by Ontario universities reported on the employment status of 1997 university graduates six months and then two years after graduation. The study was a response to announced plans by the Ontario government to introduce new "performance-indicator" regulations requiring universities to demonstrate the "employability" of university graduates by field of study. The results would have surprised those expecting to find humanities and social science graduates faring relatively poorly. The differences among academic disciplines were marginal and in many cases statistically insignificant. Six months after graduation, 93.1 per cent of Ontario graduates were employed, as were 96.4 per cent two years later. By way of illustration (see table 2 for details), in 1999, 97.3 per cent of business and commerce graduates were employed compared with 95.2 per cent for those from the humanities and 95.5 per cent from the social sciences.[26]

Other surveys reach similar conclusions – that higher education pays economic dividends, including for those in the humanities and social sciences, whose employment prospects and incomes improve markedly as the graduates age.[27]

Table 2

Employment rates of 1997 Ontario university graduates by academic program, six months and two years after graduation

Program	Six months after graduation	Two years after graduation
Dentistry	97.9	97.8
Education	95.5	99.0
Law	90.7	92.2
Medicine	92.2	100.0
Optometry	100.0	100.0
Vet. medicine	100.0	97.7
Forestry	90.9	100.0
Architecture, landscape architecture	92.3	96.7
Engineering	93.8	96.6
Business and commerce	95.4	97.3
Food science and nutrition	92.3	98.2
Theology	85.7	100.0
Journalism	97.1	97.3
Nursing	93.4	98.4
Therapy and rehab.	98.6	99.6
Other health professions	77.2	94.1
Agriculture and biol. science	87.2	93.1
Fine and applied arts	91.9	96.6
Social sciences	91.9	95.5
Humanities	91.8	95.2
Physical sciences	87.2	94.7
Computer science	90.0	93.0
Mathematics	95.0	97.3
Other arts and science	91.9	95.8
Total	93.1	96.4

Source: Council of Ontario Universities, "Highlights from the 1999–2000 Ontario University Graduate Survey," April 2000

Employment surveys that measure the university investment exclusively on the basis of short-term employment outcomes provide a partial and probably distorted view of the economic value of higher learning.

One group of graduates who merit particular attention are those with college and university instruction in the fine arts. Notwithstanding the funding pressures that cultural activities and the arts have experienced in recent years, most Canadians probably believe, or could be persuaded, that art, music, literature, film, and the theatre contribute to the health and quality of life of the communities in which they thrive. As arts patron and Vancouver businessmen David Lemon contends, "The arts are intrinsic to a sense of nation. They are intrinsic to the cultivation of a shared identity." And, he adds, "They are intrinsic to a *prosperous economy*."[28] This latter observation deserves wider acknowledgment. In 1996 the arts and culture sectors employed an estimated 670,000 individuals in Canada and contributed more than $22 billion to the Canadian gross domestic product. In the Greater Toronto area, 10.5 per cent of all employment was in the arts, constituting some 225,000 jobs and pouring about $1 billion into the local economy.[29] Canadians spent $14 billion on cultural events and activities in 1996, 27.5 per cent more than in 1986. This compared with an 18.5 per cent increase on spending in all goods and services over the same period.[30]

Notably, the artists, writers, musicians, dancers, actors and filmmakers are "among the most highly educated but least well paid workers in Canada."[31] Statistics Canada figures show that fine arts graduates from Canadian universities (1986–96) who were over thirty years of age earned an average of $17,700 annually, making them among the least advantaged in income terms of all university graduates.[32] The seasonal and contractual nature of their work, as well as the lean wages paid in this sector, account for such low individual incomes; at the same time, these graduates willingly encompass the vibrant community of creative workers that enriches the country's cultural and artistic life, not to mention its tourist industry – the world's largest economic sector. Support for the fine arts and related programs, both inside and outside institutions of higher education, appears to be a terrific economic bargain for society as a whole, a fact insufficiently appreciated by those who would slash public funding to education and culture even further. As novelist Margaret Atwood has argued, "The artist, by and large, does subsidize the rest of us ... Even when the artist does make some money, others make a good deal more."[33] A study conducted by the Toronto Arts Council found that for "every dollar of funding [of the arts] government earned back two."[34] The federal government's May 2001 injection of $560 million (over a three-year period) into the arts sector signalled a renewed interest in the cultural sector, particularly in the digitalization of the arts.[35]

Despite generally favourable employment outcomes, it would be foolish to ignore the problems that a minority of university graduates have confronted in the face of turbulent changes in the Canadian economy over the last quarter of the twentieth century. The proportionate decline of the primary industries (construction, mining, and manufacturing) and the growth of service industries (retail, financial, personal) altered the composition of the labour force. Corporate downsizing – whose victims included managers with high levels of education – and the deliberate shrinking of the public sector were triggered by debt reduction and "trade liberalization" policies intended to make the Canadian economy more competitive internationally. The business cycle fluctuated widely between 1985 and 1994, and featured both the cresting and crashing of the real estate and stock markets. In the wake of a deep recession, the unemployment rate in Canada reached 11.4 per cent in 1994, before declining slowly over the next several years.

Part-time employment grew significantly, and the economy increasingly featured a division between lucrative and rewarding "good jobs" and short-term, poorly paying, and low-skilled "bad jobs." Clearly, instability and unpredictability were the economic order of the day, and young people with low levels of education, especially in poorer regions of the country, were among society's major casualties.

University graduates were not entirely immune from these forces. Fourteen per cent of the 1995 graduating class (nation-wide) were employed part-time, and of those one-third had been unable to find a full-time position.[36] Others chose to work part-time (fewer than thirty hours per week), a common practice for women with children. Statistics Canada's 1994 General Social Survey found that some 7 per cent of university degree holders felt that their jobs were "low-skilled" (a far lower number than those with less education). It also reported that some 27 per cent of university graduates felt "over-qualified" for the occupations they held, a pattern confirmed in other studies.[37]

University graduates employed involuntarily on a part-time basis in poorly paying occupations or in full-time positions requiring minimal skills were unquestionably "underemployed." This situation, as the surveys cited above indicate, would be unlikely to continue permanently, though this probability was (and is) undoubtedly small comfort at the time. As one such BA graduate put it, "Coat-checking does involve being able to efficient ... You need the ability to keep a cool head. But pretty much any trained chimpanzee could do it."[38] A woman with a Bachelor of Education degree working as a telemarketer claimed that the only qualification for that job was the need to be patient and polite: "I haven't been able to use any of my education in this job."[39] The *Toronto Star* found other graduates in similar positions, including a twenty-nine year old with a degree in international politics and a

$45,000 debt, who bitterly anticipated a "life of underemployment" as a clerk.[40]

Sociologists David W. Livingstone and Graham S. Lowe point out that even many of the highly educated who are employed full-time in nominally skilled jobs are underutilized in their positions. In a 1994 national survey, Lowe found that while 70 per cent of employees had computer skills, fewer than 50 per cent were expected to use them in the workplace.[41] Livingstone conducted a major survey of the Ontario workforce in 1996 and determined that more than 60 per cent of Canadians of all ages and educational levels were "computer literate."[42] The youngest and the best educated were the most proficient; indeed, 100 per cent of those with a university degree between the ages of eighteen and twenty-nine had computer skills. Furthermore, Canadians enthusiastically pursue "life-long learning," augmenting their academic credentials and employment experience with additional courses and training.[43] Livingstone challenges the argument that schools and universities must, more than ever, devote their teaching resources to applied studies in such fields as business and information technology. Instead, general education should be sustained and encouraged, and the nature of work itself should engage public attention. In other words, the solution to the problem of underemployment for university graduates lies less with educators than with employers. The latter ought to understand the aptitudes of their employees better and should create environments that enable them to use and develop their skills more fully.

Strategies and policies that would improve the quality of working life for the underemployed and fully employed alike include the following: work sharing and reduced hours as a means of generating more skilled jobs; ongoing collaboration between employers and employees about the operation and direction of the organization; "encouragement of innovation based on workers' initiative and creativity"; greater recognition of employees' needs for a "balanced" life, including their child-care responsibilities; tax incentives for employers to create healthy work environments; support for employees' continuing education; and better benefit and pension plans in large and small businesses. As Graham Lowe notes, where such practices exist, productivity increases.[44] The "knowledge" economy requires inventive strategies to ensure that society has both enough jobs and sufficiently fulfilling employment. Time-worn, simplistic platitudes about the need for employees to be more efficient and better trained in more "practical" subjects do little to achieve these goals.

But don't universities have a responsibility to meet the shortage of employees in the high-technology area, which according to the software industry stood at some 20,000 unfilled positions in 1998?[45] Aren't policies designed to steer students out of the liberal arts and into applied science, therefore, sensible? University enrolments normally fluctuate by program, and over the past decade, interest in the applied sciences has grown; if attractive market opportunities in high-tech areas are sustained, further such increases can be expected. But too great a shift in university priorities and resources to the commercially driven, utilitarian areas at the expense of the liberal arts will erode the core of higher learning as defined in chapter 2, and universities will, more and more, resemble training centres with a narrow, non-academic focus.

Computer science is especially vulnerable to this orientation. Much technical knowledge, after all, has a limited lifespan. Consider, for example, the fate of computer programmers in the 1970s who believed that their expertise in the COBOL and FORTRAN programming systems would secure their positions in the industry for the foreseeable future. These systems, however, were quickly superseded by new programming methods, some of which in turn became all but obsolete.[46] Those who assume that higher education is merely about dealing with "known problems in known ways" and who therefore lack the intellectual resilience to learn new skills, cope with uncertainty, or even change fields may well be casualties in the world of employment.[47]

Indeed, it is entirely questionable whether universities have any role in attempting to respond, in a Pavlovian way, to immediate market needs, especially in such a rapidly changing field as high technology. Credible academic programs require many years to develop a scholarly literature suitable for new undergraduate and graduate teaching. Such programs cannot be started up or shut down overnight in response to immediate changes in the labour market. Community colleges or private training institutes, which do not have the same academic goals as universities, are probably better equipped to cater directly to employment demand, though students whose schooling is confined to such courses of study may well lack the general skills that liberal education offers and, as we have seen, which many (though evidently not all) employers seek.

Does it not make more sense for universities to concentrate on cultivating intellectual breadth, flexibility, autonomy, and social awareness, and for information technology companies themselves to provide the required industry-specific and ever-changing specialized skills? Graham Lowe thinks so. "Let's consider this scenario," he writes:

What if the high-tech sector put less emphasis on lobbying government for immigration-rule exemptions, or on creating strategic partnerships with universities to pump out more computer-science graduates? What if, instead, these firms tapped into the existing talent pool and trained its own staff, or graduates in other disciplines, to move into some of their vacant positions? If indeed learning and continuous innovation are hallmarks of the high-tech sector, then its businesses should create the conditions for these to take place among its workforce and new recruits. For example, firms could build on transferable skill sets in related disciplines. Students in biological science use advanced computer systems to analyze complex laboratory data; social-science students learn about relational databases through statistical software packages. Both backgrounds could be seen as stepping stones into some high-tech jobs.[48]

Not only would such strategies be likely to reduce the shortages of skilled high-tech employees, but they might counteract the much discussed "brain drain" to the United States of Canadians educated in this area. Companies operating in the United States invest far more in research and development activities than companies in Canada do, which leads to a wider array of challenging jobs for American managers, engineers, and scientists. The development of similar priorities for Canadian firms, argues Lowe, should be a major public policy issue: "That firms dependent on specific skills don't do more to develop them in-house is all the more puzzling given the high levels of general education in the Canadian labour market, which should give most workers with post-secondary education a solid foundation for expanding their skills repertoire."[49]

Overall, the labour market is far more fickle than some business and government spokespersons suggest, a fact that hinders labour market planning. Indeed, unpredictability is an endemic trait and, for many, a key virtue of "unplanned" capitalist systems. How, then, can one expect schools and universities to devise academic programs that guarantee employment in an economy rife with uncertainty, and why would politicians so committed to free market ideology (for example, those in Alberta and Ontario) require them to do so? Governments and corporations failed to anticipate the collapse of the "model" Asian economies in the mid-1990s and its reverberations in North America. Nor was the rapidity and scope of technological change itself foreseen by economic forecasters.

Indeed, for all the publicity surrounding the shortage of computer specialists, the high-technology sector accounted for
only 1.9 per cent of the Canadian workforce in 1997, and
some studies, including one from Statistics Canada, have even
challenged the claim of a recruitment "crisis" in this field.[50]
The boom and bust experience of high-tech companies on the
stock market beginning in the latter half of 2000 was but one
indication of the field's endemic volatility. The reduction of its
workforce by some 50,000 employees (half the workforce) by
the Canadian high-tech giant, Nortel, throughout 2001 was
another.[51] Overall, the economy grew impressively from 1998
to 2000, only to be confronted in early 2001 with gloomy sce-
narios about the possibility of a renewed recession. According
to one economist, "the history of attempts by government to
forecast needs for people for various types of skills does not
fill one with confidence," a conclusion borne out by a series of
erroneous "manpower" planning projections of the 1970s,
including in such applied fields as engineering.[52] Even in the
more regulated public sector, the surplus of nurses and teachers in Canada quickly turned into shortages in the late 1990s,
confounding educational planners.[53] Universities – whose
expertise is academic, not economic – can scarcely be expected to foretell employment futures more effectively than corporations and governments. Yet as we shall see more clearly in
chapter 4, this is precisely what policy makers have been
demanding, a scenario that could lead to doubly bad news:
inaccurate labour market projections, and universities shorn
of their academic and intellectual raison d'être.

Thus, for the imminent graduate of a Canadian university,
particularly those in the liberal arts, there are no iron-clad
guarantees. Employment surveys and other studies suggest
that the prospects for desirable full-time employment are
uncertain in the short term and favourable in the long term,
and that the demand for highly educated people in all fields

will continue to grow. In an unpredictable economic universe, employment conditions fluctuate, though job prospects remain the best for those with university degrees. Perhaps the only certainty is that of continuing change. Still, there are effective strategies that liberal arts (and other) students can follow in order to enhance their employment prospects, and various advice manuals contain useful information on how graduates might best approach the transition from school to work.[54]

Students are not wrong to be attentive to what they will "do for a living," and this book's purpose is by no means intended to reproach them for that concern. Quite the contrary. The link between education and "living" is precisely what this study is about; arguably, the most important contribution higher education can make to the graduate's future is to enhance his or her ability to live an enriched, rewarding life. Obtaining a job and earning a reasonable income is, of course, a significant part of this experience. So, too, is being inquisitive, informed, and engaged in the life of the mind and of one's community. Universities, in one way or another, have always carried out this mission. Ironically, even in a utilitarian age, this endeavour has proved to be at least as useful and far more durable than the host of narrowly focused, market-driven training programs so cherished by concept-challenged and culturally blinkered policy makers. Nonetheless, the skewing of higher education's function and the undermining of liberal education proceed.

4
Ideology and Policy

I s liberal education in crisis? Not necessarily, at least not yet. Students continue to enrol annually by the thousand in the social sciences and humanities. Scholarly research and publication carry on, possibly at unprecedented rates. New academic initiatives in the arts are not unknown. My argument in this book is not that the liberal arts have disappeared but that they are at risk and that if current policy trends continue in Canada, their future will indeed be in question.

This chapter identifies the source of the most serious threat to liberal education: recent government policies that privilege certain academic endeavours over others, namely, applied science, high technology, business, selected professions, and mission-oriented research, all at the expense of the social sciences and humanities, the fine arts, and basic scholarly inquiry. This tendency is reinforced by globalization, commercialization, and market forces that now steer the direction of universities as they do other institutions.

Higher education is no innocent when it comes to heeding the siren call of the economy. The Industrial Revolution in the late nineteenth century and the insatiable demand for human capital in the post–World War II period helped drive the unprecedented expansion of postsecondary education, and the liberal arts thrived through both of these eras. So what is different about the present? Essentially this: that governments are increasingly excising the universities' ability to provide broad and balanced academic programs, and the space for liberal education is shrinking. Marketplace jargon now accompanies these restrictive policies. So-called clients and customers (students) expect service providers (faculty) to enhance their economic worth in the labour market. The institutions themselves, now subjected to "performance indicators," are expected to "rationalize" their operations efficiently and, wherever possible, to "privatize" their functions. Subordinate to bureaucratic and political regulation designed to prepare students for the economy, universities may be losing the authority to fashion a future that includes liberal education. This chapter explains the process at work.

Over the course of the past two decades, universities in Canada and elsewhere have established new relationships with government and industry. From the end of World War II to the early 1970s, "social demand" fuelled the expansion of higher education. Governments provided universities with funding, enabling them to meet the enrolment pressures that arose both from the baby-boom bulge and from the popular belief that a growing proportion of young people should get a postsecondary education. The student's economic future, as well as the country's, evidently required it.

In Canada, governments used enrolment-based funding formulae (more students = more money) or block grants to universities to pay for this expansion, and the institutions generally had the autonomy to plan their undergraduate, graduate,
and professional programs. In order to avoid excessive dupli-
cation, the latter two areas normally elicited especially close
scrutiny by provincial ministries of education, and not all
requests for new programs were met. Government interest and
involvement in higher education unquestionably expanded
during this period, but for the most part academic blueprints
and priorities were drawn up by university officials or com-
missions of inquiry from which education departments took
advice. Indeed, established universities were not all interested
in growing as quickly as student demand required, and government officials had to cajole them to do so. As chapter 1
noted, given the high level of faith in the overall value of higher learning, all public investment in university and college
training could easily be justified. By the early 1970s, universities and governments had forged a "delicate balance" in the
administration of higher education, a strategy that allowed for
the emergence of diverse academic curricula, including a wide
range of liberal arts undergraduate and graduate programs
across the country.[1]

In an expanding industrial and commercial economy, business and industry played some role in the promotion and management of Canadian universities. Prominent businessmen
from surrounding communities typically dominated and
chaired the university's board of governors, which raised
money, lobbied governments, and managed the institution's
financial affairs. Normally, however, academics, led by the
president and senate, oversaw the creation and extension of
the courses of study that shaped the university's academic
identity and direction, a practice that also furnished space for
the liberal arts to grow.[2]

Nor did the private sector contribute substantially to the funding of higher education from the 1950s to the 1970s. While private donations enabled universities to support particular initiatives that might otherwise have been delayed or abandoned, public funding covered the lion's share of university expenses. Indeed, in 1970–71, while government grants nationwide accounted for 76 per cent of university operating revenues, private donations comprised less than 10 per cent. In the United States, by way of comparison, the comparable figures were 43 and 36.5 per cent, respectively.[3] Tuition fees covered the remaining operating costs in both countries and were significantly higher in the United States, particularly in private universities.

The funding of higher education in the post–World War II period reflected the Canadian tradition of supporting a wide range of social services and economic infrastructure through public finance. Rich in land mass and poor in population, Canada has historically depended on governments to fund transportation, communication, health, educational, and other projects that the private sector would not or could not sustain alone.[4] Comparable American institutions, on the other hand, were able to draw upon more abundant corporate and individual resources to create and maintain universities and colleges, though state-funded higher education was by no means absent and, as we shall see, remains prodigious. In the Canadian case, public support of universities was combined with the practice of relative institutional autonomy to allow for the evolution of diverse systems of undergraduate, graduate, and professional education. Social demand (enrolment pressures) and economic need (as we saw in chapter 3) also appear to have been met by higher education, and tuition fees were held at relatively low levels, though they were still higher than in many European countries.

Much of this changed in the 1980s with the sudden arrival

of "globalization" and the unleashing of "market" forces on educational and other institutions. A variety of factors, not all yet clearly understood, account for this shift in Canada and elsewhere. Rising expenditure debts led governments to restrain spending on health, education, and other social services and to turn increasingly to the private sector (individuals and corporations) for the provision of some of these needs. This was accompanied by campaigns by international business and government organizations such as the International Monetary Fund, the World Bank, the GATT (General Agreement on Tariffs and Trade), and now the World Trade Organization for reduced levels of taxation and a significant lowering, if not a complete elimination, of trade and tariff barriers, a development which, more than ever, expanded the business domains of powerful international corporations.[5] Heightened corporate competition led to the "downsizing"of workforces, which tended to increase a company's share value and profits while leaving many well-educated employees unemployed or underemployed. The so-called knowledge economy, generated by revolutionary changes in microelectronics and biotechnology, both facilitated the internationalization of business and raised the profile of educational sectors designed to train the personnel required by industries that depended on the use of high technology.[6] Variously referred to as neoconservatism, neoliberalism, or economic fundamentalism, the policies flowing from these changes included a growing dependence on market mechanisms for the production and distribution of goods and services that formerly lay in the public realm.[7]

For universities, the impact of these changes has been profound. The scope of higher education has simultaneously expanded and contracted. The demand for postsecondary education is now greater than ever, driven by the continuing marketability of academic credentials and by the demographic pressure of the "echo" generation – the children of baby boomers – who seek admission to higher educational institutions. But many governments now perceive the importance of higher learning in particularly narrow ways. Notwithstanding the pro-liberal arts views of some company executives (cited in chapter 3), they see little point in general education, and they are determined to make higher education a direct instrument of economic designs. Furthermore, they insist that the private sector play an active role in university and college affairs. Consider the Ontario government's educational "vision" articulated by a 1999 report of the Ontario Jobs and Investment Board: "Educational institutions and providers need to meet the needs and expectations of all their clients (learners, parents, and employers) by striving for excellence at all times, fostering entrepreneurship and innovation, and being responsive to the needs of the economy. To achieve these goals they should expand their partnerships with one another and with business."[8]

This perspective is not merely Canadian. Facing similar economic pressures, other countries have chosen to emphasize commercially oriented schooling and to "privatize" higher education further by significantly raising tuition fees. One analyst explains that higher education in Europe and North America "has evolved into a foundational component of national economic growth. It is being called upon to resolve the economic problems of nations without adequate investment in most circumstances."[9] In her examination of university policy in Australia, the United States, Britain, and Canada, Sheila Slaughter observed these patterns:

Generally, I found that all four countries instituted policies that encouraged commercial research and development and business/ vocational curricula, emphasizing the value of higher education to national economic activity and displaying a preference for market and market-like activity on the part of faculty and institutions. With regard to access, higher education policies encouraged greater student enrollment, but at a lower national cost. Rather than financing students, all countries raised tuition fees and switched from heavy reliance on grants to greater use of loans. In terms of curricula, national policies exhibited a strong preference for departments and colleges with relevance to the market. The four countries moved away from basic research toward applied or entrepreneurial research. All began integrating higher education into broad government planning processes, processes that focus primarily on economic development. In short, national policies in all four countries moved decisively toward academic capitalism, which refers to the movement by universities toward the market to secure external funds. This shift is most noticeably seen in large research universities that have developed commercial arms and links with industries to exploit intellectual capital to generate funds for universities.[10]

Doesn't the evident consensus among these nations indicate both the correctness and the inevitability of such policies? I think not. The certainty with which economic planners in the private and public sectors speak about the future ought to be questioned, as indeed it has been by certain sceptics within industry itself. It is surely a titanic leap of faith for countries such as Canada to depend on the never-ending ability of the marketplace to meet the entirety of its economic, social, and educational needs. In addition, there is reason to fear that policies designed to solve immediate economic problems – in particular, the revenue concerns of provincial and national governments – will become permanent, changing for the foreseeable future the purposes, structures, and functions of higher education. The deregulation and dramatic rise of tuition fees for graduate and professional programs in some parts of the country is one stark indication of this trend, as is the increasing requirement that universities and researchers elicit funds from private sources as a condition of receiving government grants (discussed below). As we have seen, universities have always trained people for the labour force, and market-driven academic research is hardly a novel practice. In this sense, "academic capitalism" has its own history. But the new economy cannot be permitted to completely consume educational institutions, because higher learning has broad cultural, humanistic, and social objectives that liberal education reflects and sustains. In Canada the arts, social sciences, and humanities – to say nothing of public libraries, local theatre, museums, and art galleries – have expanded, at least until recently, on the strength of general revenues provided by federal, provincial, and municipal governments.[11] Public culture still requires public funding, provided by open-minded governments that understand the benefits to individuals and communities flowing from such support.[12] To turn higher learning into a mere market commodity is to betray the generations of students yet to be and to turn our backs on the past by privatizing valuable public enterprises. Let us examine the Canadian university's place on this road, and how it might reconsider its direction.

Market-driven Policies

The erosion of public funding for higher education in Canada over the past two decades has been extensive and consequential. By withdrawing more than $6 billion from health, education, and welfare programs between 1994 and 1998, the federal government contributed significantly to the financial difficulties of institutions in all of these sectors, compounding the fiscal challenges they already faced. Provincial expenditures on higher education, measured in constant dollars, fell 12 per cent between 1992–93 and 1999–2000. To pay not only for current but increasing enrolments, universities were turning more and more to students and private donors. University revenues from government sources dropped from 74.5 per cent in 1978 to 55.6 per cent in 1998, and tuition fees rose 224 per cent between 1981 and 1998 (and especially dramatically during the 1990s). Sponsored research also accounted for a growing proportion of university funding, rising from 9 per cent of total revenues in 1972 to 17 per cent in 1997–98. Thus, while Canadian universities took in $12 billion in 1998 – the highest ever – the increase "was due almost entirely to rising student fees, income from private sources, and investment income from trust funds."[13]

The fiscal news from Ottawa improved somewhat in 1999 when the federal government announced an increase in funding to national research agencies of $150 million over three years, to be divided among the Medical Research Council, the Social Sciences and Humanities Research Council (SSHRC), the Natural Sciences and Engineering Research Council, the National Research Council, and Health Canada. One year later the government inaugurated its $900 million Canada Research Chairs program, which provided five years of funding for 1,200 senior faculty positions across the country.

These initiatives, however, scarcely reversed the policy orientation of federal and provincial governments alike, which had continually advanced the interests of disciplines believed to be vital for the "knowledge economy" over those considered less relevant. The Canada Research Chairs program, for example, assigned only 20 per cent of the faculty positions to the social sciences and humanities, despite the fact that more than 40 per cent of full-time faculty in Canada were working in these areas. The medical and applied sciences fared proportionately far better than the arts.[14] While generally enthusiastic and optimistic about the recent federal role in research funding, Robert Prichard, former president of the University of Toronto, acknowledged that "humanities and social science research has been far less well supported ... than research in

health, science, and engineering" and that the relative federal
under-investment in the SSHRC fields is regrettable and should
be corrected."[15] Indeed, a 1999 meeting of the Canadian Conference of Deans of Arts expressed "a consensus [that] the
humanities are under siege both from within their institutions
... [and] from government forces" and that "the current state
of humanities research in Canada" might be determined by
"declining humanities enrolments and federal targeted-
research funding initiatives."[16]

The bleakest scenario suggests that in the years ahead
humanities and social science programs are more likely to face
death by a thousand cuts than by the guillotine. Certain
departments in the humanities and social sciences have, in fact,
already disappeared. Facing severe provincial budgetary pressures, Université de Montréal, for example, has closed its programs in comparative literature, medieval studies, and geolo-
gy.[17] Across Canada, governments are less inclined than ever to
allow universities to control their own academic futures. In
Manitoba, recent legislation requires the provincial government to approve a university's plan to expand, alter, or termi-
nate an academic program. Alberta has introduced a new funding system, which ensures that "new student spaces will only
be opened in programs with high labour market demand."[18] In
Ontario, virtually every new dollar of public funding for higher education has been directed to projects and programs selected by the Ministry of Colleges, Universities and Training. In
1997 the province offered funding incentives to universities
that were prepared to double the number of students in computer science and engineering over three years. It also created
the Ontario Research and Development Challenge Fund,
designed to generate research for applied projects that were
able to secure private corporate sponsorship. This mirrored the
mandate of a new federal agency, the Canada Foundation on
Innovation, which has provided more than $1 billion for work

in science, health, engineering, and the environment on condition that 60 per cent of project costs are funded by the private
sector – an approach that is likely to ensure that economic
rather than scholarly interests determine the content of
research proposals.

To cope with an expected boom in higher education enrolments, Ontario offered universities and colleges $742 million
to build new campus facilities – again, with the requirement
that an equal amount be raised privately by the institutions, a
condition that seemed rather unrealistic given the historical
level of corporate funding to Canadian universities. The vast
majority of the approved building projects in Ontario's new
"Superbuild" program were in the business, applied science,
health, and information technology sectors and largely
excluded proposals from the humanities, social sciences, and
fine arts. Facing severe financial pressures as well as a skewing
of academic priorities away from the arts, universities across
Canada were depending more and more on the labour of part-
time, minimally paid, contractually limited faculty, who,
through the 1990s, bore an increasing burden of undergraduate teaching.[19]

Nothing speaks more eloquently to the practice of "academic capitalism" than the imposition of the "performance
indicator," (PI) system, a mechanism that financially rewards
the universities that best "satisfy" their customers and clients
and penalizes those that don't measure up. Superficially
rational and eminently sellable to taxpayers convinced of the
need for public "accountability," performance indicators, in
practice, are fraught with limitations. The system establishes
a number of indicators, such as graduation rates, the employment of degree holders six months and two years after graduation, graduate and employer satisfaction, and program
costs. The scheme then employs a formula for the distribution
of funding on the basis of how well each institution and its

individual programs fare in these and other categories. Such plans are defended by those who favour the market testing of universities and who seek to replace discretion in the distribution of funds with automatic formulae. In using "objective" criteria, the PI system is a current version of the "scientific management" that was employed during the Industrial Revolution to encourage cost savings and speedup in "efficiently run" factories.[20]

The criteria, of course, are anything but objective. Ontario's formula, for example, which was responsible in 2000 for the distribution of half of all new operating funds to universities, measured the employment status of students after graduation but ignored such factors as academic innovation, the quality of student scholarship, and the university's service to the community. Ann Dowsett Johnston, who has overseen *Maclean's* magazine's annual ranking of Canadian universities since 1991, described the Ontario system as "bizarre" because its criteria were so narrow and incomprehensibly punitive. For example, two years after graduating in 1997, an average of 96.4 per cent of former Ontario students were employed, and the differences between the success rates of the institutions that received PI funding and those that did not were, in a number of cases, statistically insignificant. Dowsett Johnston concluded that the system was "nothing but folly, parading in public as accountability."[21] An academic favouring the principle of PI systems also was highly critical of the criteria adopted by Alberta, Ontario, and other jurisdictions because they have attempted to simplify exceedingly complex circumstances:

While it is possible to compare universities on the employment, attrition, and loan default rates of their graduates, these do not really represent program effects or matters that are totally within the control of universities. Graduates' employment conditions are a function of the economic conditions, a contextual factor, and attrition and loan default rates are closely related to a combination of input or selection factors (the kind of students admitted) and prevailing economic conditions. Another misapplication of PI's is treating an academic's grants as the measure of research productivity or indication of his/her value to the university. This confuses grant-getting activity and contribution to the financial health of the institution with knowledge creation or generation. Some grants do not produce any new knowledge; some larger grants do not produce large amounts of new knowledge and some new knowledge is produced outside of the grant structure.[22]

Thus performance indicators, among other questionable effects, coerce universities into making academic decisions (including curricular development) on the basis of expected market conditions – betting, as it were, on the programs most likely to meet immediate economic demand. They must also expend valuable administrative capital on the endless gathering of statistics that may or may not have academic pertinence, distracting the institutions from their primary scholarly and teaching endeavours. Indeed, one report questions the degree to which legislators actually "use the mass of information supplied to them under performance reporting initiatives," an example of the so-called "garbage can model of rationality"[23] in which bureaucratic requirements generate reams of unused data. In the meantime, policy decisions flow from political or ideological considerations.

Grosjean and colleagues note the variation in PI schemes across Canada and warn observers not to generalize from the "extreme" cases of intervention into higher education by the governments of Alberta and Ontario. Indeed, the authors praise the University of New Brunswick for introducing a measurement system that credits "scholarly activity in artistic and literary creation" and requires the collaboration of faculty and administrators in establishing "appropriate institutional performance indicators."[24] Furthermore, the study contends that academics in the liberal arts could aid their cause by using PIS to demonstrate the continuing vitality and social importance of their own fields of study. The demand for institutional accountability is unlikely to diminish, and the public may well be responsive to imaginative illustrations, including quantitative ones, of the role the university plays in fostering intellectual, cultural, and democratic values.

This is possible, but the performance indicator is probably too crude an instrument to contribute much to achieving these objectives. Earlier in their report, Grosjean and colleagues note the technocratic mindset in the university that tends to accompany the introduction of this scheme. It can be considered a form of "indirect rule," in which the political authority establishes laws and regulations and then "allows" the governed to administer the system. "By using these accountability mechanisms to steer from a distance, the state ensures its performance agenda is internalized by the institution and, ultimately, by academics themselves. Thus regulation becomes self-regulation, and state control becomes self-control." Scholarly activities are then subjected to non-academic assessment criteria, making "it possible to replace substantive judgements with formulaic and algorithmic representation"[25] – an approach that is hardly conducive to the conduct of unconstrained and independent intellectual discovery.

Performance indicators exist in some form in all Canadian provinces, but one can hold out hope that their limitations will become evident to those jurisdictions still considering their expansion.[26] As of 1999, sixteen American states had implemented performance funding, and nine others were likely to do so, but owing to various deficiencies of the system, four states "had already abandoned their efforts."[27]

Another "indicator" of the growing importance of applied, market-oriented research at the expense of fundamental and curiosity-based scholarship is the recent fate of the Social Sci-

ences and Humanities Research Council (SSHRC), which is the
funding agency for liberal arts research in Canada. As of 1998,
SSHRC's budget, in real dollars, had not increased in ten years,
though applications for grants had grown significantly. Consequently, the "success rate" had dropped to one in five applicants by 1996–97. SSHRC was able to fund only 5 per cent of
the students and 15 per cent of the faculty that it represented,
and its budget was one-quarter that of the Natural Sciences
and Engineering Research Council, which provided funding to
20 per cent of its student and 60 per cent of its faculty con-
stituents. As Marc Renaud, president of SSHRC, observed, "We
are going through an extremely utilitarian period. The era of
unfettered, subsidized research is gone forever."[28]

As if to prove his point, in the mid-1980s SSHRC introduced
a program of "strategic research grants" designed to lure
scholars from the humanities and social sciences into applied
studies that address specific policy matters of "national importance." Only researchers promising to study such topics as
"education and work in a changing society," "managing global competitiveness," "exploring social cohesion in a globalized
era," "challenges and opportunities of a knowledge-based
economy," and, most recently, the "New Economy" have been
eligible to receive grants from this fund – though, again, only
one in five applicants actually do. Fortunately, "standard"
research grants from SSHRC are still available to (a minority of)
Canadian academics in the liberal arts. These applications are
subject to peer review purely on the basis of scholarly merit,
and grants are provided annually for a wide range of projects.
The loss of this fund, inadequate as it is, would spell the end
of most independent, curiosity-based research in the liberal
arts in Canadian universities. This is not imminent; nevertheless, the *strategic* grants program reflects the government's
desire to steer, rather than merely support, scholarly research.
The creation in 2001 of an unprecedented "relevance screen-

ing" process gives a committee of academics, government officials, and "senior business representatives" the power to over-
see the distribution of funds ($100 million over five years) allo-
cated through SSHRC's "New Economy" initiative.[29]

Indeed, how determined governments have been to make
universities – and their researchers – serve economic functions
was demonstrated by the report of the Expert Panel on the
Commercialization of University Research, which was
appointed by the federal Ministry of Industry, Science, and
Technology and reported in March 1999. It sought to ensure
the commercialization of "intellectual property" by obligating
all recipients of federal grants to turn their research results
over to the university, which would then be expected to find
investors to market their "discoveries." The report also recommended that universities make "commercialization" a
fourth fundamental objective of academic life, alongside
teaching, scholarship, and service, and that academics who
produce marketable and profitable research be promoted and
tenured especially quickly. In the wake of major opposition
from faculty associations and from many Canadian research
scientists who would have been expected to participate in the
scheme, these proposals were shelved by the federal government.[30] However, the "relevance screening process" described
in the last paragraph clearly, if more incrementally, promotes
the commercialization objective.

Moreover, the commercialization trend has continued on
other fronts. With federal funding, the National Centres of
Excellence (NCE) program was inaugurated in 1988, requiring
collaboration among university, government, and industry.
Research projects were assessed partly on their ability to create "new products or processes for commercial exploita-
tion."[31] The program expanded throughout the 1990s, leading to additional "partnerships" and facilitating "private
sector involvement in all network activities, including the

establishment of research priorities."[32] By December 2000, the NCE participants included 135 federal and provincial government agencies, 96 university organizations, and 567 private companies.[33]

Much of this activity could be justified by the need to improve Canada's notoriously underdeveloped industrial research capacity, and universities clearly have some role in this mission. The difficulty is that agencies such as the NCE, the Canada Foundation on Innovation, and the Ontario Research and Development Challenge Fund divert resources from basic research, whose place in both the sciences and the arts has been increasingly marginalized. Furthermore, public subsidies allocated through these programs may well be directed to many private companies that simply don't require them. In the competitive "knowledge economy," commercially promising research ought to attract investors without the need for government funds or for marriages of cash-starved universities to corporate patrons. The consequent blurring of functions between industry and higher education surely erodes the university's ability (and enthusiasm) to preserve and nourish independent scholarly research in the arts as well as the sciences.

Indeed, as Nobel Prize–winning chemist Arthur Kornberg argues, those who promote market-driven research over autonomous scientific inquiry are acting against society's long-term economic and social interests. Creative science, including biotechnology, owes its origin, dynamism, and potential to the support of *basic* research sustained by well-funded public agencies:

With regard to medical research the best plan over many decades has been no plan at all ... Investigations that seemed totally irrelevant to any practical objective have yielded most of the major discoveries of medicine: x-rays, MRI, penicillin, polio vaccine ... The breakthrough of recombinant DNA and genetic engineering, based on the discoveries of enzymes that make, break and seal DNA, were made in academic laboratories built and supported almost entirely by public funds from the public sector ... Companies are not in business to do research and acquire knowledge for its own sake. Rather they are in research to turn a profit. They possess neither the mandate nor the tradition to advance scholarship. Biotechnology companies must, instead, prove their profitability in the ebb and flow of financial markets and focus on short term goals.[34]

Corporate access to public research facilities and to academic departments brings with it influence over curricular and research programs, further compromising, potentially, the autonomy of universities. Three controversial donations from prominent business leaders to the University of Toronto in the mid-1990s were initially based on agreements that excluded language on academic freedom. In one case, the "university seemed to be granting Rotman [the donor] inordinate control over the running of the management school"; in another, the "Barrick Gold corporate advisory body" overseeing the use of donated funds was to have considerable influence over the newly formed Council on International Studies. Following campus protests, the agreements were modified, strengthening academic freedom provisions.[35]

Contract research can easily undermine a basic principle of academic freedom and liberal education – the free exchange of scholarly research. Industry contractors insist upon and usually obtain the agreement of researchers to delay publication of results so as to protect the competitive position of the "investor." As University of Guelph agricultural scientist E. Ann Clark notes, "Findings and outcomes are very often proprietary, meaning that a newly discovered protocol in genetic research cannot be used even by the lab which discovered and refined it under contract, let alone by colleagues in neighbouring labs, without the express permission of the contractor."[36]

And according to an official with the American National Cancer Institute, "As biotech and pharmaceutical companies have become more involved in funding research, there has been a shift toward confidentiality that is severely inhibiting the interchange of information."[37] From the company's commercially driven perspective, such prohibitions are understandable, but they are at odds with core academic tenets.

How much influence do donor companies wield? In some cases, an extraordinary amount. In 1998 the University of California at Berkeley signed a contract with Novartis, a Swiss pharmaceutical firm that produces genetically engineered crops. In exchange for $25 million to support basic research in the Department of Plant and Microbial Biology, the company secured "first right to negotiate licenses on roughly one-third of the department's discoveries," including projects funded by government. Novartis was also entitled to five seats on the department's research committee "which determines how the money is spent." Some 40 per cent of the faculty in the college favoured the arrangement, compared with 50 per cent who believed it would harm academic freedom. Ominously, amid the campus debate the college dean, in what some considered a "hush order," urged professors not to communicate with the media about the arrangement.[38]

Corporate-university liaisons can also lead to conflicts between the self-interest of academics and their scholarly obligations. In one revealing study, the investigators found that of 1,400 scientific and medical journals, only 210 required authors "to disclose financial ties, such as whether authors owned stock in a company whose drug they were evaluating, or had received a research grant from a competing company." A follow-up examination of these 210 journals indicated that only 0.5 per cent of the authors who had financial ties with research sponsors ("whether or not a potential conflict existed") disclosed the connection.[39] In another examination, of

789 papers in 14 prominent journals, the investigators discovered that more than one-third of the scholarly contributors had financial interests in the companies sponsoring the research they were reporting.[40] This practice is questionable enough. When researchers compound the problem by failing to declare the conflict of interest, readers can hardly be assured of their scholarly objectivity.

The *Canadian Medical Association Journal* attempted to address this problem several years ago by adopting a publication policy of trying to ensure that "only experts without ties to a drug company would be able to write editorials about a product produced by the firm." However, the editor of the journal "found it too difficult to find qualified researchers who met the requirement." He noted that there were "very few researchers in Canada that aren't doing research in one form or another for pharmaceutical companies."[41]

In a widely publicized case at the University of Toronto, Dr Nancy Olivieri, a researcher and professor, faced off against Apotex Inc., which funded part of her investigations into the experimental drug deferiprone (used in the treatment of the blood disorder thalassemia). Core financing for the project had been provided earlier by the Medical Research Council of Canada. Initially enthused about the drug's potential, Olivieri came to question its long-term effects on patients. However, a "confidentiality clause" she had signed with Apotex prevented her from publishing her critical findings without the company's authorization, a condition she later regretted and publicly challenged. She subsequently lost her position as head of the haemoglobinopathy program at the Hospital for Sick Children in Toronto, thus preventing her from continuing her clinical trials. Following a public campaign on her behalf, she was reinstated at the hospital in January 1999 and secured the University of Toronto's agreement to indemnify her against costs incurred in the event of a threatened law suit by Apotex.[42]

Growing concerns about the relationships between researchers and corporate sponsors and about the overriding
problem of conflict of interest led the International Committee of Medical Journal Educators, whose eleven members
include the *New England Journal of Medicine* and the *Canadian Medical Association Journal*, to issue unprecedented editorial regulations in the fall of 2001. Authors were now
required "to attest that they had full access to all of the data
in [the studies they were conducting] and [to] take complete
responsibility for the integrity of the data and the accuracy of
the data analysis." Journal editors were to refuse to review or
publish articles in which authors failed to "disclose details of
their own and the sponsor's role in the study" or in which
sponsors had "sole control of the data" and the right to delay
or prevent publication.[43]

This development, and the Olivieri-Apotex case[44] in particular, spoke to a number of issues: the obligation of academics to follow corporate rather than academic protocols;
the increasing dependence of universities on corporate funding of research; and the growing culture of entrepreneurial-
ism by universities and individual professors.[45] The latter tendency, a relatively recent phenomenon, has come with stern
warnings from some distinguished scholars and administrators in the United States and Canada. While generally favouring closer ties between business and universities, Derek C.
Bok, the former president of Harvard University, expressed
these reservations:

It is one thing to consult for a few hundred dollars a day or to write
a textbook in the hope of receiving a few thousand dollars a year. It is
quite another matter to think of becoming a millionaire by exploiting
a commercially attractive discovery. With stakes of this size, the
nature and direction of academic research could be transmuted into
something unlike the disinterested search for knowledge that has long

been thought to animate university professors. In short, the newfound concern with technology transfer is disturbing not only because it could alter the practice of science in the university but also because it threatens the central values and ideals of academic research.[46]

Though scarcely typical, the tragic events at Montreal's Concordia University in 1992 led to an investigation and exposure of problems arising from that institution's entrepreneurial culture. Accusing several individuals of appropriating his scholarship and hindering his career advancement, Valery Fabrikant, a member of the Department of Mechanical Engineering, killed four of his colleagues, wounded one secretary, and was subsequently sentenced to life imprisonment for murder. Invited to investigate the standards of "academic and scientific" integrity at Concordia, a commission headed by Harry A. Arthurs (a legal scholar and former president of York University) found that at least some of Fabrikant's charges were legitimate. Among other problems, senior academics had indeed attached their names to publications essentially produced by more junior scholars. And faculty with "copious academic credits and large contracts generally enjoyed financial support for their research, prestige, and influence. This privileged access to resources in turn allowed them to continue publishing while others were denied the means of becoming more productive."[47]

Such unhealthy practices were not unique to Concordia. According to the Arthurs report, they were increasingly common in Canada and arose from a "political economy" that emphasized a "production system of research" in which publications served as the "unit of currency." In this atmosphere there were hazards: "the risks of undermining primary responsibilities for teaching and academic research, the risk of succumbing to the temptation to engage in undesirable procedures, to falsify results, even to engage in fraud."[48] These were not the inevitable results of the emerging relationship between the university and the marketplace. But as the Concordia and other cases have demonstrated, self-interest, conflict of interest, and commercial competition have the potential to warp academic culture.

One could argue that, abuses aside, commercially oriented academic work, *by definition*, subverts a basic precept of liberal education in that research contracts between academics and external sponsors inevitably encumber, in some way, autonomous intellectual inquiry. Furthermore, the "community" which universities and professors serve is limited in these arrangements to those interests that can afford to purchase an academic's services. As E. Ann Clark observes,

Compare the $700 million currently spent annually by the federal and provincial governments [much of which requires matching corporate funding] to support genetic engineering with the *virtually undetectable* amounts allocated to support *organic farming* as an alternative to capital- and resource-intensive production practices (including herbicide-tolerant crops); *management-intensive grazing* as an alternative to growing animal grains (e.g. corn and soybeans) to support confinement feeding systems; or the design of *small-scale production* cooperatives to supply local foodsheds as an alternative to dependence on long distance transport of imported foods in Canada ... The absence of well studied and documented benefits for non-proprietary technologies [– which arises from] the scarcity of research funding – obliges [agricultural] producers to continue along the path charted for them by industry, for the benefit of the industry.[49]

However, if one accedes to the reality, and increasing incidence, of academic-corporate associations, universities should at the very least be vigilant in defining and enforcing the conditions that permit these relationships. This is to ensure, as fully as possible, the integrity of academic life. Indeed, private sponsorship, in the arts as well as the sciences, can in fact enhance scholarly endeavour, by serving as a catalyst for basic, socially responsive, or medically valuable research that might not otherwise elicit support. But it is imperative that information about such projects be open and that ethical concerns be transparently addressed.

Contract terms between researchers and external sponsors should be entirely public. Academic staff should control the direction of research and the reporting of results, and corporate interests should have no editorial control over published texts. Delays in publishing findings about commercially viable products should be minimal and strictly adhered to. External organizations should have no involvement in the appointment of faculty to academic departments. Professors and researchers should be obligated by universities to report any financial interests they have in the companies that support their academic activities. Graduate students, whose research is frequently funded by private agencies and corporations, "should not be channelled into work that is potentially profitable but not educationally valuable,"[50] nor should they be deterred from pursuing research that sparks their curiosity, whatever its potential market value. Safeguarding the autonomy and virtue of universities and academics in the face of pervasive, market-driven research will not be easy. But the costs to university education will be high if this is not achieved.

The continuing privatization of postsecondary schooling poses yet another challenge to liberal education. Higher education in Canada remains overwhelmingly in the public sector, though private universities, under fairly restrictive conditions, are permitted to function in several provinces. The Government of Alberta recently provided the Devry Institute of Technology with degree-granting powers, and in December 2000 the Ontario government passed legislation that would allow both non-profit and for-profit private universities to be established and to offer degrees. These institutions would receive no capital or operating grants, but their students would be entitled to the same level of provincial financial assistance as those in publicly funded universities. A government memo in November 1999 explained that private universities "could be helpful in meeting student demand in addressing special situations in a manner that would not create fiscal pressures."[51] This suggests that private universities are foreseen as a mechanism for coping with expanding enrolments that would otherwise generate additional funding for public universities. The legislation would also enable the minister to permit Ontario's community colleges to offer Bachelor of Arts degrees and to become universities. The first of these, the Ontario Institute of Technology (an outgrowth of a local community college), is designed explicitly to offer "market-driven programs."[52] Thus, little-known private universities and vocationally oriented colleges might well enhance their status by offering BAS, but the "flooding" of the market with such credentials would surely diminish the value and perceived distinctiveness of a liberal arts degree from traditional universities.

Some people hope that private higher education will lead to the establishment of "Harvards of the North," that is, prestigious and well-endowed universities that would offer academic competition to the educational "monopoly" exercised by publicly funded institutions. The former, at least, is highly unlikely, just as it was several years ago when the Ontario Council on University Affairs, a government advisory body (since abolished), investigated the issue, held public hearings, and rejected the private university option. It argued that "even a relatively wealthy jurisdiction like Ontario is not able to support high quality private institutions without recourse to some level of public assistance," and it noted that "in nearly half of the states in the United States, private institutions are given some help by state and local appropriations."[53] The council predicted that, legislation permitting, small religious colleges and business and technical institutions would be the first off the mark to establish themselves as degree-granting universities.

The council may have been prescient. A quickly expanding private university – founded in Arizona, now operating in British Columbia, and likely to be authorized in Ontario – is the University of Phoenix, which specializes in business and technology-related programs, and whose quality of education has been widely questioned in the United States. With some 60,000 students who are, typically, working adults, it employed in 1998 only140 full-time faculty (with heavy administrative responsibilities) and 5,100 part-time instructors, or "practitioners," 90 per cent of whom had jobs elsewhere. No one has tenure, faculty research and scholarship are of little consequence, and the university has no actual library on any of its campuses. Instead, it uses a "Learning Resource Centre" in which students have access to electronic on-line journals. In addition, they use the library resources of other (including publicly funded) universities. Students can earn their degrees on-line. Those attending full-time in British Columbia pay $40,800 for an undergraduate degree, which is economical by American private university standards but more than double the cost of an average Canadian degree. Such cost-efficient educational practices are evidently profitable. The University of Phoenix is a publicly traded company and earned some $46 million in 1998.[54]

In all likelihood, private universities in Canada, at least for a time, will have difficulty attracting large numbers of students willing (or able) to pay such high fees, though if tuition costs continue to climb in public universities, this situation could change. Nor will private institutions soon be in a position to offer the range of programs available in existing Canadian universities (let alone at Harvard). A study of for-profit universities in Australia found program choice to be "limited" and focused on business-related subjects. "No research is required of teaching staff, nor is there any expectation of community service."[55] David Strangway, the former president of the University of British Columbia, has chosen a different strategy from that of the University of Phoenix and Unexus, a new "on-line" university. He is planning to open in 2002 a private liberal arts institution in Squamish, British Columbia, that will charge annual tuition fees of $25,000. If successful, this university may well serve the cause of liberal education – but in traditionally elitist ways, catering in all likelihood to a small number of students from especially well-endowed families.[56]

Still in an embryonic phase, private universities in Canada are not yet a realistic alternative to publicly supported higher education. But their presence is a symbolic statement by provincial governments that the marketplace will play a growing role in the affairs of higher learning. The message is that if potential students seek business or information-technology training instead of liberal education, universities should meet this demand. If credential-hungry students prefer Internet courses that can be completed in relatively short periods of time, these too should be provided. Otherwise, "upgraded" colleges or private universities may, deservedly, capture more of the education market than universities. In a more competitive, commercially driven environment, universities should take nothing for granted – not the financial support of government or business, not the idealism (vs the pragmatism) of students, and not the future of the liberal arts.

A related challenge to the autonomy and traditions of Canadian universities arises from Canada's participation in the North American Free Trade Agreement and the World Trade Organization. The WTO was established in 1995 to further the process of liberalizing international trade by eliminating government regulations in business. The WTO permits member countries to design policies for services such as health and education that lie within the public realm. Thus, government subsidies to public universities are perfectly acceptable. However, once educational institutions (as well as health care establishments) are exposed in a significant way to market forces, protective policies may no longer be possible.

The greater the degree of privatization and commercialization in these sectors, the more vulnerable they are to challenge by foreign "competitors" seeking "fair" (i.e., similar) treatment. Private institutions, such as the University of Phoenix, could then claim that they, like public universities, should receive government subsidies. Alternatively, they could demand that public universities should lose their grants and face market pressures on the same basis as their private competitors. The former scenario is more likely, leading to an unintended consequence: expected by some governments (Ontario, for example) to offset the need for additional public funding to higher education, private universities could cost the system even more. Alternatively, existing higher educational budget allotments could simply be divided into smaller portions, resulting in a transfer of public revenues to private institutions – institutions distinguished thus far by high tuition fees and low levels of interest in the liberal arts.

Furthermore, as economist Marjorie Griffin Cohen observes, "If Canada agrees fully to cover educational services under the existing GATS [General Agreement on Trades in Services] rules, those rules would require that foreign educational service providers be guaranteed access to the Canadian educational market."[57] Philip G. Altbach, an expert on higher education systems internationally, contends that in a deregulated universe in which higher education is included in the "group of commodities under the control of the World Trade Organization," developing societies will lose the ability to shape their educational futures: "Higher education ... is dominated by the world-class universities in the industrialized countries – which are also home to the leading multinational corporations in information technology, biotechnology, and publishing. The norms and values of those countries crowd out other ideas and practices."[58]

Supporters of private universities, market-driven learning, and a much-diminished public sector believe that Canada would be well advised to emulate the American example where competitive, privately funded education is wide-spread.[59] The United States certainly has a long history of private higher education. Nevertheless, 80 per cent of American students attend public, state-funded colleges and universities, so this system is (and for the last 140 years has been) an essential cog of American higher learning.[60] Furthermore, unlike in Canada, state financing is increasing in the United States. According to the Council of Ontario Universities, between 1995–96 and 1999–2000, total public funding of Ontario universities (not adjusted for inflation) fell by 8 per cent and it fell by more than 4 per cent in the other nine provinces. By comparison, state funding of universities in the United States rose by an average of 28 per cent over the same period.[61]

Canadian libraries have fared especially poorly in comparison to those in the United States. If library resources have at least some effect on the quality of liberal – and other – education, Canadian universities are facing significant challenges. The Association of Research Libraries (ARL) ranked 110 university libraries in Canada and the United States with respect to such factors as "volumes held and volumes added during the previous fiscal year." It found that with the exception of the University of Toronto, every Canadian library included in the study fell in ranking between 1992 and 1997.[62] And while ARL member libraries in the United States had budget increases that averaged 31.3 per cent over that period, the funding of Canadian member libraries declined by 3.4 per cent. Thus, Canada might well be advised to emulate the American example, not because the United States has reduced public support for higher education in recent years (as neoconservatives imply) but because it has done precisely the opposite.

One consequence of the financial uncertainty, the bureaucratization of university life, and the spread of "white-collar unionism," especially in the public sector, has been the growth of campus unionization by full-time and part-time faculty. Some 50 per cent of university faculty in Canada had joined unions by the mid-1980s. By campaigning for the preservation of academic freedom and against the commercialization of higher education, campus unions can play a useful role in limiting the impact of market-driven pressures on academic programs and institutional priorities. Furthermore, they can be effective representatives of faculty (particularly sessionally employed part-timers) who seek reasonable wages and benefits. It is scarcely surprising that employer-employee relations have been especially confrontational in an era of provincial and federal budget cuts in the educational sector.[63]

However, in the discourse and collective-bargaining strategies they employ, academic unions, unintentionally and ironically, contribute to the "corporatization" of campus life. When an adversarial "industrial" model of management-labour relations is transposed to the university site, the environment conducive to rational, civil intellectual inquiry can be impaired. In especially contested cases, where dialogue between administrations and faculty associations breaks down, strikes can occur. Such events can themselves provide rich educational material for teachers and students, but in my experience – and I work at a university (York) that within a four-year period (1997–2001) endured an eight-week strike by full-time faculty and an eleven week strike by part-time faculty and teaching assistants – they are more likely to induce hostility, frustration, and cynicism, especially among students, who generally view their disrupted classroom experience as a burden to be endured rather than an educational experience to be cherished.[64] Unconstrained managerialism on the one hand and militant unionism on the other fuel power struggles that can spoil the climate required to sustain liberal education.

One final worrisome observation: if, as I argued in chapter 2, contemporary liberal education includes service to the community, and if an accessible university is an important component of such service, then Canada, of late, has taken a regressive step. Statistics Canada reports that "while the university participation rates for young people from low and middle SES (socio-economic status) backgrounds were quite similar in 1986 – 13.7 per cent and 14.5 per cent, respectively – by 1994, a wide gap had occurred between these two groups, with the rates standing at 18.3 per cent and 25.3 per cent, respectively."[65] Thus, in a period of steep increases in tuition fees (126 per cent from 1990 to 2000, six times the inflation rate),[66] those from especially modest backgrounds were having greater difficulty in attending university than those from more advantaged circumstances. A study of the family origins of University of Guelph students confirmed this pattern. The proportion of low-income students attending the university declined markedly between 1987 and 1996.[67] In light of the fact that the average debt load of students in Canada graduating with four years of postsecondary education rose from $9,000 in 1990 to an estimated $19,000 in 1998–99, this is perhaps not surprising.[68] At the University of Western Ontario Medical School, the marked rise in tuition fees from $4,844 in 1998 to $10,000 in September 2000 appears to have had an immediate impact on the social class profile of the students. Over this period the average family income of students climbed from $80,000 to $140,000.[69] Whether the federal government's new "millennium scholarship" program will have any effect on access patterns remains to be seen.

The scenario described in this chapter, if not in the entire book, is unquestionably bleak, but as I suggested at the outset, it would be alarmist to proclaim that liberal education is on the verge of vanishing from the Canadian university. Notwithstanding the restructuring and reorientation of higher education, liberal arts enrolments remain strong. It is indeed the case that in Ontario between 1988 and 1998, applications for places in the arts declined by 28.5 per cent compared with an increase in engineering by 27.5 per cent, and that across the country, student enrolments in history, economics, geography, political science, and languages declined markedly during the 1990s.[70] Nonetheless, nationwide, some 58 per cent of all university degrees granted in 1994 were in the social sciences, humanities, and fine arts, compared with 57 per cent in 1998.[71] (By comparison, in the United States 20.7 per cent of university and college degrees were in the humanities in 1966 but only 12.7 per cent were in 1993.)[72] So long as students seek liberal education, then universities and governments, so attuned to market demand, would be ill-advised to close down or dramatically shrink programs in these areas.

A more immediate challenge is to ensure that the quality of the liberal arts is preserved. Huge classes (taught primarily by teaching assistants and poorly paid part-time faculty), diminishing library resources, minimal research funding, inadequate government support to universities with less and less independence, and academic and research agendas driven increasingly by commercial interests, all cheapen higher learning and erode its scholarly foundations. In these circumstances, liberal education might endure, but to what end? Students may obtain their degrees, but what will their credentials signify? – If nothing else, that higher education can be delivered efficiently en masse in a way that preserves liberal education in name only. Furthermore, if large numbers of retiring faculty in the social sciences, humanities, and fine arts are not replaced, and if the lion's share of new funding from public and private sources continues to flow to the professions and applied fields, then within a decade the character and orientation of Canadian higher education will have been significantly transformed.

The concerted efforts to make universities a mere "subsector of economic policy" ought to be rethought.[73] Educators and policy makers should understand that higher education is not equipped to lead or save economies, or even to accurately anticipate long-term labour force demands – a challenge that, to date, has confounded business and government themselves. By continually attempting to meet expected market needs, thereby raising public (and private sector) expectations, Canadian universities will pay a price: they will be penalized for failing to rescue the country when economies turn down. The history of higher learning suggests that the greatest contribution universities can make to society is to ensure that high-quality liberal education thrives, a task more vital than ever in a world that appears to value matter over mind.

5

Teaching and Learning

The health of liberal education depends not only on the enlightenment or folly of government policies but also on academics themselves. It is not sufficient for me and my colleagues to bemoan the actions of external authorities who seek to shape and redirect the university in the constricting ways described in the last chapter. We must also take responsibility for what goes on inside our own classrooms. This does not mean merely denouncing students for being uninterested in the stimulating intellectual content we provide for them. In fact, we are not consistently interesting, and students may have good pedagogical reasons for tuning us out and preoccupying themselves with final grades instead of course material. But aren't students now worse than ever? Don't they typically think, speak, and write incoherently? Some do, but some always have, a fact that nostalgic, aging professors usually forget or overlook. A minority of students perform brilliantly, and most, as always, lie between the two academic extremes.

Today's students share many characteristics of their predecessors, but like every generation, they are distinctive in certain respects. Teachers in the liberal arts as well as in other fields ought to know something about the culture, values, and expectations of their students if they expect the classroom to be a lively and engaging place. Teaching techniques that worked twenty-five years ago may not be as effective today. For example, students have come of age in the era of the computer and the Internet, whereas professors have adapted, at times with difficulty, to the new technology. How should it be employed, if at all, in the humanities and social sciences? Is it merely another instrument of academic commercialization, or can it serve the cause of liberal education? This chapter probes such questions. In admittedly broad strokes, it attempts to identify the students, to probe aspects of popular culture that affect academic life, to offer examples of creative teaching methods, and to encourage faculty to be reflective and self-critical rather than hectoring and condescending in their discussion of teaching and learning; in other words, to examine classroom instruction through the lens of liberal education.

In the 1930s, according to the principal of Queen's University in Kingston, Ontario, his institution provided an undergraduate program so appalling that it "would not elevate a cow," a problem evidently mirrored in American colleges and universities, where at least half the students, allegedly, were "not educable." They could "neither see, nor hear, nor think; they ha[d] no disposition to work, nor capacity for sustained effort." Universities, according to some critics, were "places where pebbles were polished and diamonds dimmed." Similar complaints could be heard about the quality of students and higher learning in every era, including our own. In *The Great*

Brain Robbery (1984) three historians claimed that Canadian universities "were on the road to ruin" because its students were overwhelmingly and increasingly mediocre, an assessment they repeated in 1997 in *Petrified Campus: The Crisis in Canada's Universities.*[1] Such caustic writing is part of a distinctive genre in the literature on higher education, and if all such works were to be assembled and taken literally, one would have to conclude that since the Enlightenment, and probably earlier, most students, including graduates, have performed abysmally, and universities have not only tolerated but encouraged this intellectual sloth.[2]

Students' most severe critics are usually professors who habitually base their opinions about the continual decline of academic work on anecdotes, personal experiences, and general impressions. Persuasive, systematically gathered evidence in support of such views (like that required in student essays, for example) is infrequent, in part because it is exceedingly difficult to make a reliable comparison of the quality of students across generations. Would declining grades and high failure rates over a given period indicate deteriorating scholarship or higher standards? In order to test results validly, shouldn't sociology students in one era be required to complete exactly the same assignments and tests as those of another era? Even if this were done in specific disciplines, how could one account for and measure the student's understanding of *new* knowledge? Supposedly "objective" tests are themselves the product of their times, privileging some information and erudition over other data and perceptions. Scholarly principles accepted as conventional wisdom in one period may be disproved and dismissed in another.

In the 1920s and 1930s, for example, respected academic journals published articles derived from the now discredited theory of eugenics, which purported to prove the intellectual inferiority of women, certain immigrants, and people of colour.[3] Student essays that might have received a first-rate grade sixty years ago for arguing in support of eugenics would not likely fare so well today, even if they were engagingly written. Should one now assume that researchers today are smarter than in the past, or that the culture itself is more tolerant and discerning as a result of social changes originating outside the university? In light of these complexities, blanket statements about the diminishing quality – or conversely, the progressive improvement – of students in the liberal arts or any other field ought to be treated sceptically. We can, however, confidently conclude that academic culture and student life have changed over time, as has the identity of the student constituency itself, but whether students are better or worse remains, for the most part, a question of speculation.

This is not an argument for ignoring the issue of academic performance. Professors, after all, do regularly assess, compare, and grade student work, and certain opinions and evidence, selective and partial as they are, cannot easily be ignored. For example, a new and reasonably systematic study of seven Ontario universities found evidence of significant grade inflation in recent years. Between 1973–74 and 1993–94, final grade-point averages in eleven of twelve first-year subjects rose markedly. The authors had no clear explanation for this phenomenon. However, they doubted that students in the 1990s were better than those in the 1970s, and they hypothesized that instructors had, over time, become "more generous."[4]

In 1996 twenty-two Ontario professors signed a letter to the *Toronto Star* which claimed that university students "are less and less able to comprehend the same books; less and less able to listen attentively ... less and less aware how to prepare for an exam, write a paper, research a subject in the library."[5] These views may well have been another example of mere impressionism or professorial grumpiness. At the same time, as *Petrified Campus* observed, universities in the 1990s were commonly providing "remedial courses in English or French" for students who had graduated from high school without university-level writing skills.[6] (How many such students was and is unknown.)

Intelligent as they may be, students – particularly graduates – who cannot express themselves effectively are scarcely articulate voices for the cause of liberal education. Greater attention to this problem at all levels of the educational system ought to be encouraged and welcomed so long as curriculum demands designed to improve student performance are sensible as well as exacting. Ensuring that students, year in and year out, develop their writing skills through continual practice is valuable and necessary. Doing so in reasonably sized classes where individual attention is the rule not the exception enhances the instructional process.

Standardized tests, now increasingly common in elementary and secondary schools throughout North America, do contain significant writing and comprehension components, but these examinations are not the magic literacy bullet that some believe them to be. Critics point to the unrealistic cognitive expectations placed on young children by these tests, their failure to probe the learner's creative and abstract thinking skills or to assess the true abilities of English-as-second-language students, and the arbitrary nature of performance categories used in ranking the tested students.[7] Standardized testing may be another politically popular "performance indicator" in an educational environment now preoccupied with training and measurement. But if otherwise bright students fail to make the requisite grade on tests that measure certain kinds of aptitudes and not others, their commitment to schooling may diminish, not increase.

Testing, new core curriculum requirements, and other "reforms" are in part a response to public disenchantment with the "progressive" educational initiatives introduced in the 1960s and 1970s. Child-centred classroom approaches were not an unqualified success and have certainly merited reconsideration.[8] But contemporary policy makers in schools and universities ought not to throw the baby out with the bathwater. Those institutions genuinely interested in cultivating a student's autonomy, resilience, intellectual breadth, social awareness, critical thinking, and communication skills (see chapter 2) should understand that one educational size does not fit all. For students to thrive, discipline and examinations should be combined with (not replace) flexibility, innovation and creativity in the classroom. Traditional teaching methods based mainly on memorization, frequent testing, and other quantitative assessments may satisfy the current craving for educational "accountability," but on their own they insufficiently cultivate the life of the mind.

If professors understand that they cannot take for granted consistently outstanding work from their students (hardly a shocking or novel realization) and that academic vigilance is ever necessary, what else should they know about the people who inhabit their classrooms? Although researchers have paid relatively little attention to the question of student values and concerns, it is possible to fashion a portrait of the identity and beliefs of the contemporary university student.

Earlier we noted the growing diversity of North American students by gender and cultural origin, itself a justification for schools and universities to attend thoughtfully to the complexities of a multifaceted community, both inside and outside the classroom. More than ever, students from divergent backgrounds expect to hear their voices and see their images reflected in academic study, something now made possible by emerging literature in the humanities and social sciences. Instructors will also find themselves managing classroom discussions among these students involving the subjects of gen-

der, religion, and race. The tensions that arise from such seminars can either be a source of intellectual stimulation and genuine learning or the cause of anger and classroom mayhem.
Enlightened academic departments and university programs
devoted to improving teaching can provide faculty with a
forum to discuss their experiences and concerns around these
issues, and to learn techniques for effectively guiding conver-
sations on controversial subjects.

Are students in fact interested in controversy and debate –
core components of liberal education? Notwithstanding wide-
spread interest in the issues of race and gender, surveys conducted over the past decade in Canada and the United States
indicate that university students tend to be more pragmatic,
more vocationally oriented, and more politically conservative
than those of the previous generation.[9] Many faculty, especially those who came of age in the turbulent 1960s, lament
such conventional attitudes, which are reflected by students'
apparent preoccupation with grades and careers rather than
ideas and social issues. This, however, oversimplifies the picture. Students are unquestionably job-oriented, but other educational matters concern them as well. A survey at one Canadian university found that while 84 per cent of students were
motivated to attend by career-related concerns, fully 81 per
cent wanted a good general education.[10] Another examination
of first-year student attitudes at seven universities in Canada
similarly concluded that "students go to university both for
intellectual development and in order to prepare themselves
for the job market after graduation."[11]

Furthermore, while many students may have intended to
come to university for vocationalist or materialistic reasons,
American research of the 1970s and 1980s found that they
became more interested in the intellectual aspects of their education as they proceeded through university: "Compared to
freshmen, seniors attach greater importance to the value of a

liberal education and less importance to the value of a college education as a vocational preparation." Seniors also put more emphasis on the "intrinsic characteristics of a job," such as intellectual challenge and autonomy, and less on its "extrinsic rewards," such as salary and job security.[12]

Students are not as one-dimensional in their beliefs and interests as some observers contend. Like earlier cohorts, they shape their values and identities out of the world in which they live, which of late has been a challenging, unpredictable place. Since the mid-1970s, economic uncertainty, rapid technological change, rampant consumerism, high divorce rates, and political cynicism have all influenced youth culture. The philosopher and professor Mark Kingwell characterizes campus life in this way: "The students who come to my institution, in their various colours and their awkward postures, are a mass of contradictions and conflict. Their identities, their very bodies, are battlefields in the modern culture wars. They come from many places and traditions, and they enter a world with its own traditions, some of them bizarre, but still loosely held together by the idea that rational inquiry is basic to human life ... Out of these materials, shifting and variable, they must construct something called an identity."[13]

Some students focus on the ends more than the process and content of university education, while others are inquisitive, ingenious, searching, or lost. There are students who thrive on the individualism and anonymity of mass education but more who seek meaningful contact in their classes and encouragement from their instructors. What do they find most challenging about university life, according to surveys? Managing their time and completing their assignments in light of financial pressure (including ever-rising tuition fees), part-time jobs, and family responsibilities. Today's students, who come from social backgrounds ranging from very affluent to exceedingly modest, take little for granted, view things sceptically, and perceive university education as the key to a good job and a rewarding life.

There are elements of these aspirations and experiences that echo through the ages and others that are unique to this era. My own experience – and here my comments will be sinfully but briefly impressionistic – is that undergraduate students, especially in first year, are curious, relatively open-minded, and anxious to draw from their professors' knowledge and guidance. They are, for a time at least, in awe of the university and quite prepared to engage the world of ideas. Professors, indeed, may be insufficiently aware of the influence they wield among students in these initial academic encounters. (The least interested and interesting students are those who are merely filling an elective requirement in the arts and are far more focused on their business or computer science programs.) In the upper years, as students become more secure and somewhat more cynical, they learn how to complete written assignments more efficiently while often appearing more detached and less involved in classroom discussion than professors would like.

But I have also found that such students are reachable, able and willing to devote themselves to intellectual life if instructors are pedagogically imaginative and personally approachable. Lecturing tediously and conducting seminars in preachy, patronizing, or intimidating ways are counterproductive intellectually, and faculty who do so hamper liberal education. Arts courses taught drearily by professors who make no effort to engage students, and which offer no venue for discussion, contribute less to liberal education than vocational training that successfully elicits students' ideas and creativity. Students in one study were asked to describe the qualities of professors nominated for teaching awards. The latter were found to be "intellectually exciting," concerned, accessible, encouraging, challenging, and dedicated to teaching.[14]

Familiarizing themselves with contemporary learning styles can enhance the classroom experience for faculty as well as students. One researcher contends that the majority of today's students succeed best in an academic environment based on "direct, concrete, experience, moderate to-high degrees of structure and a linear approach to learning." However, the majority of faculty are inspired by the "realm of concepts, ideas and abstractions"; they wrongly assume that students, like themselves, favour a high level of individual autonomy in their academic work, and they generally depend on passive forms of classroom learning.[15]

Rather than simply decrying this state (assuming it has some validity), faculty can, through effective liberal education instruction, help bridge the gap between themselves and students. The latter seek clear, detailed instruction in assignments and helpful feedback in grading, and professors can provide these without compromising their academic ideals. More than in the past, students are oriented to group learning, which, if effectively practised, can enrich the discussion of ideas and concepts. Initial assignments can be based on concrete events and then move in a logical fashion to more abstract notions, thus presenting "experience earlier, theory later." To sustain students' interest in the liberal arts and to teach more effectively, two authors suggest that faculty should "learn more about who their students are, how they learn, and how they may be taught."[16]

Some professors have had good success with an approach called "constructive controversy," in which students are systematically taught to debate ethical, philosophical, and topical issues. Working in small groups, they prepare and present their cases, then switch sides, all in aid of encouraging informed argument, critical thinking, and rational discussion. The students search for, without always achieving, an intellectual synthesis from competing perspectives; where differences endure, protagonists have a fuller appreciation of each other's views.

After three decades of using this method, practitioners have found "higher-level reasoning strategies, the development of more complex and coherent conceptual structures, and more critical thinking." Students "read more library materials," probe issues more deeply than those taught in more traditional ways, and display and acquire "an understanding and appreciation of diverse points of view." The authors conclude that such teaching practices "leave an imprint" on students: "From the way students act at the beginning of a class, we can tell a great deal about the professors who taught them previously. Whether your students sit passively and are interested only in what will be on the test, or volunteer their conclusion and engage in spirited disagreement, you know a great deal about who taught them before."[17]

A related example of creative pedagogy is Frederick Stirton Weaver's notion of "critical inquiry" teaching, which emphasizes the "habits of mind" of students more than the task of accumulating information – the "trivial pursuit" approach to learning now so popular among some back-to-basics educators. The author agrees with Robert Hutchins's contention that "the mind is not a receptacle, information is not education. Education is what remains after the information taught has been forgotten. Ideas, methods, habits of mind are the radioactive deposits left by education."[18] Therefore, teachers should "develop students' abilities to use logic, evidence, and sense of context to identify the role of selection, premises, and perspective in other people's analyses and to construct and defend interpretations of their own. In other words, students must engage self-consciously and critically in the construction of meaning."[19] Weaver believes, controversially, that all students should take a course in statistics, first so that they can learn how to present information clearly and coherently but, more importantly, in order to come to a critical appreciation of how statistics can be manipulated. They could explore how data categories are created and assembled, what unstated assumptions underlie this process, and how the same data can produce conflicting results. "Interactively," students would critically examine one another's use of statistics. The value of this knowledge, academically and socially? Not only would it encourage "systematic" and discerning thinking, but in a world flooded by information, it ought to contribute to informed citizenship. It would also increase the numeracy skills of liberal arts graduates, something found to be lacking in those seeking employment in the private sector.[20] Finally, it might enliven what is notoriously the dullest subject in the liberal arts.

Problem-based learning, pioneered at McMaster University Medical school in the 1960s (see chapter 2), can also work well in humanities and social science courses at both undergraduate and graduate levels. Cooperatively, students explore a particular issue in depth – its social, intellectual, cultural, and scientific dimensions – and teach their classmates about the subject. The professor, non-intrusively, plays a mentoring role and virtually never lectures. "Numerous instructors at all levels report that classrooms come alive, that absenteeism drops dramatically, and that no one falls asleep in class. The students are encouraged to take charge of their own learning and are assisted in developing the skills to do so."[21]

Though liberal education purists may find the concept objectionable, cooperative learning, which combines classroom instruction with occupational assignments, can be an effective teaching method, especially for students interested in quickly linking higher learning to the "real" world of employment. Arts programs at a number of universities, including my own (York), sponsor work placements for students in such fields as mass communications, urban studies, and labour studies, thus underlining the links between theory and practice, and providing participants with valuable workforce experience. The Department of History at the University of Ottawa has placed students not only in archives and museums but also in such agencies as the Ministry of Revenue. Officials there apparently like history students because they write well and know how to ferret out information.

Similar programs exist in a number of American universities. At Wichita State University, for example, some 250 students in the Liberal Arts and Sciences College are placed each year in jobs related to their majors. Social science students generally work in social agencies such as Big Brothers and Sisters, correctional settings, adoption centres, women's crisis centres, and law offices, while humanities students are assigned to cultural institutions such as museums. Math and natural science students work for actuaries or for various businesses with an environmental focus. The university perceives these programs as an important part of its strategy to exploit the institution's "metropolitan advantage" and to raise its profile within the community. Students invariably speak highly of these atypical educational experiences.

However, simply creating a structural link between students' liberal education and a stint in the workforce will not alone enhance their academic and employment experiences. If the work is mundane, treated as a mere recess from the classroom, or perceived by professors and students alike as a barely tolerable credit requirement, then the value of the exercise is questionable. Researchers have found that the most effective forms of cooperative education are those which faculty strongly support; in which students are encouraged to apply concepts and skills learned in the classroom; and in which they are able to assess critically their work experience in the light of academic theory.[22]

John Dewey, the influential American educational philosopher, favoured such a form of educational "pragmatism," which his critics later misrepresented as an enthusiasm for mere vocational training that eschewed intellectual work. Dewey in fact deplored such a dichotomy. He wrote that "the fundamental unity of the newer philosophy is found in the idea that there is an intimate and necessary relation between the processes of actual experience and education ... Growth, or growing as developing, not only physically but intellectually and morally, is one exemplification of the principle of continuity."[23] He believed in the classical Greek educational ideal, which cherished "a sound mind in a sound body," and thought this could be achieved by the deliberate melding of scholarly study with practical experience. One without the other was inadequate. "Essentially, he argued that vocational education must be provided in a form that stressed its 'liberal' aspects," something that high-quality co-op teaching can provide.[24]

A unique placement program exists in the College of Humanities at Carleton University in Ottawa. The college offers a select number of high-achieving students a set of courses that cover, in thematic form, the fields of literature, languages, philosophy, and religion. Designed to contribute to the development of the "whole person," the curriculum explores "myth and symbol" in the first year, "reason and revelation" in the second, "culture and imagination" in the third, and "science, technology, and power" in the fourth. The program then places students in internships with businesses and community organizations (from law firms to non-profit agencies such as Amnesty International) where employers and employees can, ideally, witness and experience the mutually enriching relationship between intellectual and working life.[25]

A more traditional liberal arts program, without a placement component, can be found at Concordia University in Montreal. The Liberal Arts College offers a degree course in "Western Society and Culture" to small classes of some fifteen students and two professors who participate in "animated" discussions of twenty to twenty-five books a year. According to one graduate, "The extensive and intensive education it offers is essential to the development of the contemporary thinking person, one endowed with social awareness, acumen and open-mindedness ... Meanwhile, my friends sit in jam-packed auditoriums at other Canadian universities, religiously listening to a single professor preach his point of view and rarely getting the opportunity to question it."[26]

The Imperial College of Science, Technology and Medicine in London, England offers a final example of innovative, interdisciplinary teaching, involving some three thousand students each year. Designed in the early 1970s to offset the tendency to excessive academic specialization in the arts and sciences, the plan was inspired by the traditional Greek ideal of achieving balance in education and life. It stresses the importance of exploring scientific issues in social and cultural contexts and considers "some of the central moral, political and social issues of contemporary society." Courses address both technical and conceptual questions and may include a problem-solving and/or work placement component. Ideally, technical expertise combines with community service. In one case, students designed a strategy to improve the operation of a Meals on Wheels service, and in another their work led to the establishment of a sheltered workplace in a London borough.[27]

It is important, then, for university instructors to assess regularly the effectiveness of their teaching, to be self-critical, to consider their own ability to sustain a meaningful intellectual community with their students – in other words, to employ the tools of liberal education in managing their own classrooms. One question that no professor can any longer escape is the role that new technologies ought to play in higher education. Does the wired universe enhance or devalue higher learning? What, if anything, can the bells and whistles of the World Wide Web contribute to liberal education, whose raison d'être is the fruitful and distinctly non-automated exploration of ideas? Academics are clearly divided on this issue, a subject that would scarcely have been discussed less than a decade ago. Proponents of electronic teaching are increasingly influential, as "virtual" universities compete with traditional institutions now offering on-line courses. Canadian participation in this endeavour is growing. In 1999, Canada provided 16 per cent of the 12,500 Internet courses available internationally.[28]

Typically, students who register in on-line programs appreciate the convenience of working from their homes in their own time, freed from inflexible, institutionally based teaching schedules. This is the wave of the future, according to Linda Harasim, a Simon Fraser University professor who directs Canada's Telelearning Network of Centres of Excellence, which coordinates on-line teaching initiatives throughout North America. Reversing epoch-long patterns, the campus will increasingly come to the student, who will "have access to powerful, enjoyable, effective learning environments wherever [they] are and whenever [they] have time to learn."[29]

By opening previously untapped or unavailable intellectual sources, the Internet can enrich the content as well as the form of university teaching. Indeed, most academics will by now have had the experience of browsing the Web and discovering research and teaching materials that used to be inaccessible or unknown. Paintings and other images from galleries or museums, commentaries on the writings of ancient scholars, archival documents, course syllabi from academics teaching in similar fields, and connections with new-found colleagues around the world all demonstrate the educational potential of the Internet. As Burton Clark notes, scholarly communities and identities now cross institutional and national boundaries in previously unimaginable ways, a process advanced by computer-based communication.[30]

Faculty who use Web sites and e-mail in their teaching claim that students who are too shy to speak in seminars, or who remain unknown to professors in large lectures, now find their voice. They pose questions, engage in discussions with their classmates, and provide an ongoing written record of their progress in the course. In general, students enrolled in such courses work more independently outside the traditional classroom structure, a skill that should encourage lifelong learning, according to champions of the distance education method.[31]

To date, as a University of Illinois investigation of Internet teaching found, on-line courses focus more on training and paraprofessional than on highly academic education. Working adults who seek credentials or upgrading in work-related fields constitute most of the University of Phoenix constituency, as noted in the last chapter. According to a full-page newspaper advertisement, Royal Roads University in British Columbia aims its distance education program at "mid-career professionals who want to advance their careers through graduate studies, while balancing the demands of family and work."[32] Business training is especially popular on-line and is evidently a lucrative source of revenue for universities providing it. Duke University, for example, offers a nineteen-month executive MBA, which combines Internet and classroom training, for a cost of $85,000, often paid for by employers. Even the venerable Oxford University provides a two-year certificate computer science program on-line in which students are required to spend one week on campus and to take their final exams there.[33] In 1999, Dalhousie University in Halifax began an on-line master's course in electronic commerce, and other Canadian universities have taken similar initiatives, which, according to a report for the Council of Ontario Universities, is only the beginning: "It is our collective conviction that the strategic harnessing of these new technologies will ultimately not only help to produce graduates who are better suited to the many and diverse demands of today's society but also help to enhance their learning experience."[34]

There is, however, another side to the story, told most urgently by David Noble, a historian of technology who teaches at York University in Toronto. In a series of three articles, titled "Digital Diploma Mills" (circulated first, ironically, on the Internet), Noble rejects the "technology-as-progress" argument. He sees Internet teaching as the most recent incidence of educational "commoditization," a process designed to fully integrate higher education into the market economy and to facilitate the corporate appropriation of "intellectual property." The reform of the 1980 patent law in the United States gave universities "automatic ownership of patents resulting from federal government grants." In response, many universities turned more of their resources towards research rather than teaching, hoping to take economic advantage of the new law. Simultaneously, government funding for the operation of universities shrank, leading to higher tuition fees, larger classes, and the recruitment of many more untenured part-time faculty – patterns also evident in Canada. University dependence on private corporate funding consequently increased, bringing with it many of the questionable contractual arrangements discussed in chapter 4.

Electronic teaching now promises even greater efficiencies by reducing the number of full-time faculty. If universities own the copyright of on-line courses produced by professors (an issue that is currently the subject of legal battles), then these courses can subsequently be "taught" by part-time instructors. Universities are huge markets for the new technology, making them especially vulnerable to the enticements of corporate giants offering research funding, endowments, and sponsorship of business-friendly (including on-line) curricula in exchange for access to faculty and student purchasers. Educational institutions and academics (usually in the liberal arts) refusing to yield to these pressures are deemed elitist, irrelevant, and out of sync with the needs of the global economy.[35] The message is clear: universities which fail to embrace the high tech universe, which confine themselves to teaching liberal education, and which employ traditional instructional techniques exclusively are likely to fade away. As one distance educational coordinator in California lamented, "the vendors are putting the pressure on," and many universities, with minimal planning, are jumping on the Internet-course bandwagon.[36]

Notwithstanding the enthusiasm of "techno-zealots" who envision a wired (or wireless?) world more diverse and democratic than the present one, history offers a sobering lesson with respect to the educational use of technology. Similar promises were made, and unfulfilled, in the wake of other "revolutionary" technological innovations. As one group of sceptics recalls, "Education policymakers have careened from one new technology to the next – lantern slides, tape recorders, movies, radios, overhead projectors, reading kits, language laboratories, televisions, computers, multimedia and now the Internet – sure that each time they have discovered educational gold. Eventually, the glimmer always fades, and we find ourselves holding a lump of pyrite – fool's gold."[37] Somehow, nothing has managed to render personal interaction between professors and students obsolete. The machines may become outmoded, but people never do.

Fool's gold or precious metal: What *is* the educational worth of the new technology? As the University of Illinois study suggested, there are elements of truth in all of the conflicting claims cited above. The Internet is potentially a remarkable resource, but not inevitably so. For one thing, contrary to popular belief, the costs of on-line teaching are high, especially in liberal arts courses that require close faculty-student interaction. The University of Illinois report concluded that, "with rare exceptions, the successful online courses we have seen feature low student to faculty ratios. Those rare exceptions involve extraordinary amounts of the professors' time ... Sound online instruction is not likely to cost less than traditional instruction ... Any transition of 'efficiency to quality' comes with a high quality price tag."[38] Student "consumers," therefore, ought to be suspicious of high-tech companies and universities that employ few teachers and show impressive profits while promising "first-rate" electronic teaching.

Internet courses may well be an effective way of delivering information to large numbers of students, which likely explains their growing popularity in certain applied and technical fields, but this "hydraulic" model of instruction scarcely qualifies, by any credible definition, as liberal education.[39] The World Wide Web is nothing more or less than a massive source of information that must be sifted, scrutinized, and processed. As with any traditional educational sources – library books, academic journals, government documents – students require guidance and feedback as they prepare essays and other course assignments. Computer-based learning appears to work best when it augments, rather than replaces, proven instructional methods. Faculty and students alike can use the Internet to introduce the class to interesting course materials; course listserves (e-mail networks) can facilitate communication; assignments can be more easily turned in. Learning, certainly, can go on simultaneously in actual and virtual classrooms.

The latter venue, however, has certain risks. A non-discriminating student lacking appropriate (and time-consuming) faculty oversight will have difficulty distinguishing between the credible scholarly information and the rubble that clutters the Internet. The opportunistic, dishonest student will find plagiarism easier than ever. The convenience of on-line teaching notwithstanding, lacking personal contact, professors will find it difficult if not impossible to get to know their students as individuals. Non-verbal communication (obviously impossible on-line) is an important dynamic in seminars, where instructors can creatively respond by drawing out quiet students or amending teaching approaches.

One could argue, legitimately, that in huge lecture courses, faculty and students remain strangers. But if classes with 400 or more students are the result of government funding cuts, the employment of academic "efficiencies," and increasing privatization (including the luring to campus of companies selling high-tech instructional products), then the proposed "solution" of on-line instruction flows from a self-fulfilling prophecy. It addresses a teaching problem, but for the "marketization" of higher learning need not have been created in the first place. A conventional Latin warning comes to mind in a world now inundated with educational hardware and software: *Caveat emptor.*

But in the face of such powerful economic and technological forces, isn't it futile to attempt to preserve, let alone revitalize, liberal education? If young people read too little, watch too much television, and spend countless hours surfing the Web and playing computer games, don't they come to university already incapable of exploring broadly the "life of the mind?" It would be naive to deny the impact of popular culture, particularly the new media, on children and adolescents. But despair, nostalgia, and age-old clichés about wayward, lost youth add little of value to the discussion. They are reminiscent of moral panics in earlier eras about the frightening effects on the young of novels, the cinema, comic books, (the back seats of) automobiles, and rock and roll. All too typically, the president of Dalhousie University in the 1930s deplored popular fads which, he claimed, threatened social mores and intellectual life: "In no generation have there been such stunning distractions from study" as "movies, comic strips, jazz music and other alleged amusements."[40]

Such comments were almost always based on speculation or moral outrage, not on systematic study. There is no shortage of research today on the effects of television viewing, though it is controversial and contradictory. Some studies show that creative programming sparks the child's curiosity and helps develop his or her reading ability. Other researchers warn of the impact on children and youth of continual media exposure to "violence, inappropriate sexuality and offensive language."[41] Common sense, in addition to academic research, suggests that those who spend excessive periods watching television or using computers are impairing their physical health, their social development, and even their educational progress.[42]

But as in the past, it is certainly possible to exaggerate such "dangers." Teenagers spend less time in front of the television than their elders. According to Statistics Canada, in 1998 adolescents age twelve to seventeen watched TV an average of 15.9 hours per week, compared with 22.3 hours for the population at large.[43] And rather than being consumed and conditioned by television, young people frequently approach it passively, quizzically, or irreverently. One study found that adolescents prefer spending time with peers than with television and that girls especially combine TV viewing with other activities such as visiting friends, doing household chores, or listening to music.[44] Few young people avoid TV completely, but it is hardly the all-embracing, intellectually corrupting leisure activity that some worried adults believe it to be. Pointing to the extraordinary increase in the number of children's books published from the 1970s to the 1990s, *Maclean's* magazine discovered a "Kidlit Boom" in Canada in 1995.[45] The recent phenomenal success of the Harry Potter series by British author J.K. Rowling is surely a reassuring sign that children and youth can still be turned on by reading.[46]

For Hal Niedzviecki, a young Canadian writer, the instruments of pop culture are in fact a potential source of creativity that educators at all levels would be well advised to comprehend. The new media are ubiquitous and inescapable, says the author in a compelling and eloquently written book, but young people do not expect the video industries to provide moral or educational lessons, nor do they take their content or images literally. Many *are* fascinated by process and presentation and are "knowingly drawn into a medium (television) that can flash up to one hundred images a minute into our brains. And what a minute! Sixty seconds pulsing with the kind of artifice that makes life interesting. Style and attitude, colour and glamour, nonsensical truisms and completely sensible lies ... [Many] watch television for its capacity to disgust, horrify, reveal, and penetrate the thin veneer that covers up the heart of darkness deep in the jungles of the post-industrial experience." Approached in this way, the media can inspire innovative and critical thinking, writing, and production. "Since birth," notes Niedzviecki, "we've navigated the highways of mass culture. We know how to communicate and interpret those conventions, and we are coming to realize that we can use them, rather than be used by them ... So we take our culture into us and regurgitate it in forms that attempt to return to us the privilege of speaking for and to ourselves."[47]

University students have similar goals to youth through the ages: the desire to express their ideas and individuality and to shape their identities, to create authentic cultural forms, to be taken seriously *and* to entertain themselves, to prepare for and ultimately engage in interesting post-university work. The venues and media through which these goals, and liberal education itself, are pursued have certainly evolved. Students are not taught to give speeches as they were in Ancient Greece and Rome. They are not consumed by theology or scholastic study as in the Middle Ages, or by notions of definitive knowledge as contained in the Great Books of the 1940s, though elements of all these educational forms still have a place in the university.

So, too, do the new media. Rather than lamenting this reality or belittling the interests of those who occupy their classrooms, professors should aim to know their students and whence they have come. The dialogue that flows from this discovery is the key to effective liberal education in this – or any – era.

Conclusion: Educational Futures

Whither the contemporary university? Consider this scenario for the year 2015. Dependent for some 90 per cent of their income on a combination of private funding and tuition fees (now approaching $20,000 for a BA in Canada), higher educational institutions (including colleges and universities) are explicitly mandated to meet prescribed functions. These include providing targeted numbers of graduates for particular employment sectors, which are determined at regular intervals by oversight committees consisting of industry, government, and university officials. Public funding is entirely contingent on performance indicators, such as the employment success rate of academic programs and employer and student satisfaction. Provincial governments pay a far lower share of higher educational costs than in the past, but they retain legal authority over the administration of the system, including the power to license degree programs. Private, for-profit institutions are permitted to compete for public resources with their non-profit counterparts.

Universities and colleges have niche responsibilities: some are designated as applied science institutions for the training of biotechnologists, engineers, computer scientists, and other communications specialists; the health sector trains doctors, dentists, pharmacists, optometrists, nurses, physiotherapists, and home-care workers; a third group prepares skilled employees for the construction, automotive, and other mechanical trades; a fourth educates future teachers, social workers, and child-care workers; a fifth, the administrative sector, consists of business and law schools, which train entrepreneurs, managers, and administrators for work in private and public companies and organizations; finally, an arts sector offers programs in such fields as the fine arts, literature, philosophy, politics, economics and history.

In each academic faculty, "partnerships" with organizational sponsors are encouraged, and eventually will be required. In exchange for continuing financial support, companies may appoint representatives to serve on recruitment, curriculum, and other administrative committees. Programs are assessed on a regular basis in terms of their "market" responsiveness. Each new course has a three-year trial period; those failing to attract appropriate numbers of students and those whose graduates are deemed unable, in sufficient numbers, to find employment in the fields for which they were trained will be closed down. On-line teaching is increasingly the norm in higher education. In order to obtain adequate funding for traditional on-campus courses, departments must demonstrate why such curricular offerings could not be more effectively taught on the Internet. The ratio of part-time to full-time faculty (the former do almost all of the on-line teaching) has increased to 3:1 across the country.

Following the practice in private, for-profit institutions, tenure is being replaced by renewable contracts for full-time faculty. As a result of changes in most provincial labour laws, faculty no longer have to pay dues to campus unions, a development that diminishes the unions' influence in the few institutions that still have them. In order to attract full-time faculty in a competitive international market, salary scales are higher than in the recent past.

Finally, in each province, there is one designated research institute in the sciences and arts whose members, chosen from among the county's most renowned scholars, are freed from teaching responsibilities in order to conduct research on a full-time basis. Research priorities for the institutes are set by boards of directors consisting of government, industry, and academic representatives, who are mandated to allocate resources to those projects designed to advance the country's (or individual province's) economic and social development. Core funding is provided by federal and provincial governments. Academics with private sponsorship and/or marketing arrangements for their discoveries can expand their research facilities and earn higher incomes.

Readers may view this scenario as alarmist or, depending on their educational perspective, promising. Certainly, such a system would require significant change, from province to province, in the structure and administration of higher education. Yet as I have attempted to demonstrate throughout the book (especially in chapter 4), there is nothing in this vision incompatible with changes that are already underway in Canada and elsewhere. Higher education, more than ever, *is* market-driven, the influence of private industry has grown, public funding is down, and tuition fees are up. The educational distance between colleges and universities, and public and private educational institutions is narrowing. For many influential people, the raison d'être of postsecondary education is its measurable value in the global economy. Through their regulatory powers, governments are compelling universities to enter the marketplace and abide by its rules. As chapter 1 pointed out, higher education has always played an important role in training graduates for the labour market – but not to the point of virtually excluding the cultivation of intellectual life through liberal education.

Of course, the above scenario preserves a small space for the liberal arts. But in the ubiquitous world of "academic capitalism," the humanities, the social sciences, the fine arts, and curiosity-based research in the sciences and arts would have to prove their market-worthiness, attracting students and corporate sponsors in competition with high-flying educational competitors who have some distinctive commercial advantages. The liberal arts would, in all likelihood, constitute a diminished part of the university curriculum.

It is possible, following from the discussion in chapter 5 of creative teaching and learning approaches, that professional and vocational educators would see the wisdom of grounding their graduates in all of the skills that liberal education, at its best, provides. Thus, liberal education could survive even if the liberal arts were marginalized. But the pressure to train for the labour force quickly and cost-efficiently, particularly in light of institutional competition, would probably minimize the time students would have for general, broadly based, culturally informed, or interdisciplinary education. Instead, they would be steeped in an exceedingly narrow form of vocational instruction.

Is it too late to ensure the integrity of higher learning by sustaining and strengthening its intellectual core? Is the project of providing liberal education to something other than a selected minority doomed? I think not, though I am not as sanguine as some analysts. Burton Clark, an American scholar who has written extensively on higher education, believes that the very complexity and fragmentation of a system of market-driven colleges and universities allow more opportunity than ever for academic diversity: "In an evolution that is natural for adaptive species, systems move toward more niches rather than fewer."[1] He anticipates the continuing growth of universities and academic specialties, integrated not by single institutions but by communication networks that span borders and help create international communities of scholars with shared interests. In this vision, academic opportunities in all fields, including the arts, multiply rather than diminish.

Similarly, the British author Ronald Barnett stresses the creative possibilities arising from "supercomplexity" in higher education, a condition characterized by "uncertainty, unpredictability, challengeability and contestability." Drawing in part from postmodern theory, he contends that the traditional university has already passed out of history and it is inconceivable that any unifying, universal principles or strategies can re-establish it. "The knowledge explosion ... produces an ignorance explosion," he claims, making the world "radically unknowable." The task of higher education is to prepare people to live with uncertainty and to explore every conceivable facet of the human condition, contingent as this accumulated knowledge might prove to be. Interdisciplinarity is essential in this brave new world: "The university may have no clear legitimizing purpose, no definite role, no obvious responsibilities and no secure values. Never mind: all kinds of new opportunities are opening up and will continue to do so if the university can position itself cleverly. The university is dead; long live the university."[2]

I believe that while these authors identify certain creative, even chaotic, tendencies in contemporary academic life, they understate the ways in which market forces impose a distinctive and palpable uniformity on higher education. The commercialization of intellectual property, the competition for corporate funding, and the imposition by governments themselves of what Barnett calls "performativity" criteria combine to diminish the place of liberal education, whose utility in the "real" world continues to be in question. The precipitous decline of the proportion of American students graduating in the humanities since the 1960s is but one indication of the direction of higher education, and this in the world's largest, most diverse, and most market-driven system of colleges and universities.

Even so, the cause of liberal education is not yet lost. As I noted earlier, the majority of university students in Canada still enrol in the arts, and the public system of higher education has not yet been fully privatized. Some wealthy patrons from the private sector continue to talk positively about the arts, and even fund them periodically. Some innovative teachers in the applied sciences and professions value interdisciplinarity and encourage critical thinking. Furthermore, the impressive success of the CBC television series, *Canada: A People's History*, suggests that public interest in the world of ideas can be tapped and encouraged, notwithstanding the attraction of alternative forms of popular culture. The latter, too, as I intimated in chapter 5, can also be hardy grist for the academic mill.

While I agree with those like Bill Readings[3] who contend that universities can no longer be instruments of singular cultural ideals, liberal education can still cultivate attitudes and skills that enhance individual and community life. Intellectual autonomy, resilience, critical thinking, a balance of broad and specialized knowledge, tolerance, community participation, and effective communication are scarcely obsolete aptitudes, and it is difficult to understand why these core aspects of liberal education (as discussed in chapter 2) should ever be considered unimportant or irrelevant. Furthermore, applied learning, professional education, and vocational instruction that fully embrace these concepts are superior to practical training in which they are absent. By adhering resolutely to the values of liberal education and the scholarly practices that flow from them, universities can secure the ballast that will steady their course in a sea of relentless change. Without such ballast, higher education may well be adversely, unrecognizably, and permanently transformed.

Notes

CHAPTER I

1 Rothblatt, "The Limbs of Osiris," 22.

2 Kimball, *Orators and Philosophers*, 17.

3 Plato, *The Laws*, cited in Cohen and Garner, *Readings in the History of Educational Thought*, 11.

4 Mitchell, "From Plato to the Internet," 18.

5 Kimball, *Orators and Philosophers*, 13.

6 Ibid., 46.

7 Domonkos, "History of Higher Education," 9.

8 Following an affair and secret marriage to Héloïse, one of his students, Abelard was castrated by agents of her uncle and exiled to a monastery. Héloïse was sent to a convent and the two never saw each other again. Their subsequent written correspondence sheds light on their personal struggles and is the basis for the recounting of one of history's poignant love stories.

9 Noble, *A World without Women.*

10 Brubacher and Rudy, *Higher Education in Transition,* 114.

11 Kimball, *Orators and Philosophers,* 167.

12 Miller, *As If Learning Mattered,* cited, 75.

13 Carnochan, *The Battleground of the Curriculum,* chapters 1–3.

14 McKillop, *A Disciplined Intelligence.*

15 Cardinal Newman, *On the Scope and Nature of University Education,* 83.

16 Ibid., 99. For a detailed study of evolving notions of professionalism, see Gidney and Millar, *Professional Gentlemen.*

17 Bledstein, *The Culture of Professionalism,* and Axelrod, *Making a Middle Class.*

18 Cited in Woody, *A History of Women's Education in the United States,* 76.

19 Orton, *The Liberal Education of Women,* 43.

20 Hutchins, *The Higher Learning in America,* 85.

21 Jasen, "Educating an Elite," 269–88.

22 Horn, *Academic Freedom in Canada,* 172–7.

23 Rudolph, *Curriculum,* 189.

24 Harris, *A History of Higher Education in Canada, 1663–1960,* 522.

25 Kimball, *Orators and Philosophers,* 196.

26 For a discussion of university cooperation in the "war" against un-American (allegedly communist) activism, see Schrecker, *No Ivory Tower.* On Canada, see Whitaker and Marcuse, *Cold War Canada.*

27 Jasen, "In Pursuit of Human Values (or Laugh When You Say That)," 247–71.

28 Bloom, *The Closing of the American Mind,* 346.

29 Nussbaum, *Cultivating Humanity.*

30 For an account of such a major conflict in Canada, see Marchak, *Racism, Sexism, and the University: The Political Science Affair at the University of British Columbia.*

31 Both cited in McKillop, *Matters of Mind*, 41–2.
32 Veblen, *The Higher Learning in America*. Underhill cited in Axelrod, *Making a Middle Class*, 81.
33 See Axelrod, *Scholars and Dollars*, for a fuller discussion of this process.
34 Rothblatt, "The Limbs of Osiris," 63–4.
35 Readings, *The University in Ruins*.
36 Ibid., 185.
37 Ibid., 192.

CHAPTER 2

1 For a penetrating analysis of these intellectual currents in the nineteenth century, see McKillop, *A Disciplined Intelligence*.
2 Anderson, *Prescribing the Life of the Mind*, 55.
3 Ibid., 58.
4 Freedman, *Idealism and Liberal Education*, 2.
5 See Gidney and Millar, *Professional Gentlemen*; Collins, *The Credential Society*; and Larson, *The Rise of Professionalism*.
6 Jansen and van der Veen, "Adult Education in the Light of the Risk Society," 125.
7 Anderson, *Prescribing the Life of the Mind*, 103.
8 Kingwell, *The World We Want*, 43.
9 Schafer, "Medicine, Morals and Money."
10 Vanderleest, "The Purpose and Content of a Liberal Education," 12.
11 Wagner, "A Subtle Tyranny," 328, 336, 339.
12 Little, "Multiple Goals in Liberal Arts," 346, 349.
13 Miller, *As If Learning Mattered*. According to the author, Hutchins agreed with Richard Kimpton, his successor as chancellor of the University of Chicago, that the Great Books program was "superficial and shallow" (87).
14 Precisely such a "multidisciplinary studies" program exists at the University of Massachusetts-Dartmouth in which arts stu-

dents can include science courses in their degree studies. See Leamson, "Learning without Majoring In It," 336.

15 "Evolution of Engineering Education in Canada," 1–2.

16 Association of American Colleges, *Liberal Learning and the Arts and Science Majors,* 2: 89–90. See also White, *Essays in Humanistic Mathematics,* and American Association for the Advancement of Science, *The Liberal Art of Science: Agenda for Action.*

17 Lowell et al., *Final Report of the Commission on Medical Education,* 24.

18 Nuland, "The Uncertain Art," 124.

19 Woodward, "Monitoring an Innovation in Medical Education," 27–8.

20 Towle and Jolly, "Case Studies," 42.

21 Wasylenki, Cohen, and McRobb, "Creating Community Agency Placements for Undergraduate Medical Education," 380.

22 Ibid., 382–3.

23 Gilbert et al., *From Best Intentions to Best Practices*, 44; O'Heron, "Different Students, Different Needs."

24 For fuller discussion of this issue, see McKillop, *Matters of Mind,* and Axelrod, *Making a Middle Class.* On the United States, see Levine, *The Opening of the American Mind.*

25 Granatstein, *Who Killed Canadian History?*

26 Fekete, *Moral Panic,* 214. See also Emberley, *Zero Tolerance.*

27 For an account of such incidents, see Horn, *Academic Freedom in Canada,* and Schrecker, *No Ivory Tower.*

28 Nussbaum, *Cultivating Humanity,* 19.

29 Bond, "The Arts That Liberate," 140.

30 Institute for Higher Education Policy, *Reaping the Benefits,* 18.

31 Nesteruk, "Business Teaching and Liberal Learning," 56–9.

32 Sorger, McMaster University, cited in *Toronto Star,* 15 December 1997.

33 Howes, "Ethics as More Than Just a Course," *National Post*, 28 October 2000, D4.
34 Canadian Education Statistics Council, *A Statistical Portrait of Education at the University Level.*
35 In 1996, among university graduates, 64.8 per cent of students in fine arts, 57 per cent of those in humanities, and 53.2 per cent of those in the social sciences were women. Canadian Association of University Teachers, *Bulletin Online* 44, no. 9 (1997).
36 Kett, *The Pursuit of Knowledge under Difficulties.*
37 Selman and Dampier, *The Foundations of Adult Education in Canada.*
38 Harris, *A History of Higher Education in Canada, 1663–1960,* 456–7. The veterans' participation doubled university enrolments in Canadian universities between 1944 and 1948.
39 Statistics Canada, "Adult Education and Training."
40 Schuller and Bostyn, "Learners of the Future," 78–95.
41 Shorris, "On the Uses of a Liberal Education," 50–9; "Course Teaches Humanities for the Poor," *Vancouver Sun*, 29 February 2000; "Plato and Poetry for the Poor," *National Post*, 15 July 2000; Alphonso, "School of Hard Knocks Mixes Plato, Poverty," *Globe and Mail*, 6 January 2001; Shorris, *Riches for the Poor.*
42 Cited in Fulford, "Canadian Science Writing Undernourished, Inferior."

CHAPTER 3
1 Cited in *National Post*, 11 February 2000.
2 Francis, "Universities Grabbing Too Big a Slice of the Education Pie."
3 Galt, "More Prefer College to University: Poll," *Globe and Mail*, 22 June 1999, A5. The question: "People sometimes argue about whether it is best for young people to learn a trade

or skill, or to get a good general education. Generally speaking, do you think young people should be encouraged to go to community college or university?"

4 Acharya, "University Won't Beat College Diploma: Poll," *Toronto Star*, 15 July 1998, E3. The question: "What do you think would be the most valuable type of education to have in the work force 10 years from now: College diploma in technical occupation, apprenticeship in a skilled trade, university degree in science, high school education and lots of on-the-job training, professional graduate degree such as law/social work; university degree in arts?"

5 Toronto Board of Trade, *Beyond the Status Quo*.

6 Godsoe, "Universities Must Excel Despite Less Funding," 44.

7 Rushowy, "The CEOs Artfully Intervene," *Toronto Star*, 8 April 2000, A1; and Allard et al., "Hi-Tech CEOs Say Value of Liberal Arts Is Increasing."

8 MacKinnon, "Arts Degree under the Gun," *Toronto Star*, 27 April 2000, J2. For other examples, see Garrison, "Business Loves the BA," 30, 33.

9 Stueck, "Non-techies Stake Claim." *Globe and Mail*, 19 April 2000.

10 Useem, "Corporate Restructuring and Liberal Learning," 18–23.

11 Das, "New Economy Craves Graduates with Arts Degrees, Congress Told," *Edmonton Journal*, 27 May 2000, B4.

12 Appearance on "Special Feature on Higher Education," *Studio Two*, TVOntario, 4 September 2000.

13 Hersh, "Intentions and Perceptions," 16–23.

14 Useem, *Liberal Education and the Corporation*, 63.

15 Oblinger and Verville, *What Business Wants from Higher Education*, 22.

16 These included the ability to "communicate, manage information, use numbers, think and solve problems, be adaptable, learn continuously, and work with others." See Conference

Board of Canada, "Employability Skills 2000+."

17 Useem, *Liberal Education and the Corporation*, 28–33, 123–37.

18 Paju, "The Class of '90 Revisited," 9–29. For a summary of
several National Graduate Survey reports, including that of
1995 graduates two years after graduation, see Human
Resources Development Canada, Applied Research, *Bulletin*,
Special edition, Summer 2001.

19 Axelrod, Anisef, and Lin, "Against All Odds?"

20 Allen "The Employability of University Graduates in the
Humanities, Social Sciences, and Education: Recent Statistical
Evidence," discussion paper 98–15, Department of Economics,
University of British Columbia, 1998, 30. The paper is avail-
able through Adobe Acrobat, at
www.educ.ca/wrnet/working%20papers/wps99-02.pdf.

21 In 1995, 70.6 per cent of university graduates who were 25–29
years of age were in professional/managerial positions, 7.7 in
clerical positions, 10.5 per cent in sales, 6.9 per cent in service,
and 4.3 per cent in blue-collar occupations (Allen, "The
Employability," 49, table 4).

22 Allen, "The Employability," 8.

23 Ibid., see table 7, "Managerial and Professional Occupations
by Field of Study, 25–29 Year Olds, 1991," 52.

24 Ibid., 25. See table 8, "Annual Income of Women by Education
and Field of Study, 1991," 53, and table 9, "Annual Income of
Men by Education and Field of Study, 1991," 54.

25 Krahn and Lowe, *1997 Alberta Graduate Survey*, 46, 48.

26 Council of Ontario Universities, "Highlights from the
1999–2000 Ontario University Graduate Survey." The survey
included 19,614 graduates, representing 45 per cent of the
class of 1997. A previous survey of 1996 graduates was published in 1999. The nationwide unemployment rate for those
with university degrees had fallen to 4.3 per cent by 1999
(Little, "Canadians May Have to Shed Gloom on Jobs Front,"
Globe and Mail, 21 April 2000, 2).

27 See Grayson, *Experiences of York Graduates – Two Years Later*; Guppy and Davies, *Education in Canada*, 158–62; and Anisef and Axelrod, "Universities, Graduates and the Market Place," 103–14. Michael Useem confirmed this pattern in an earlier American study, *Liberal Education and the Corporation*, chapter 4.

28 Quote from 1993, cited in Canadian Conference of the Arts Web site www.culturenet.ca/cca/quotes.htm, 2000 (my emphasis).

29 Toronto Arts Council Web site, <www.torontoartscouncil.org/> 2000.

30 Cromie and Handelman, "Consumption and Participation in the Culture Sector," 1–5.

31 Canadian Conference of the Arts Web site, <www.culturenet.ca/cca/artfacts.htm> 2000.

32 Axelrod, Anisef, and Lin, "Against All Odds?"

33 Quote from 2000, cited on the Canadian Conference of the Arts Web site <www.culturenet.ca/cca/quotes.htm> 2000.

34 From Toronto Arts Council, *The Cost of Cutting*, cited in Valpy, "Cuts to Culture Confirm Old Economic Thinking," *Globe and Mail*, 13 March 1999.

35 Scoffield, "$500-Million Arts Plan Boosts Internet Culture," *Globe and Mail*, 3 May 2001, A1.

36 Carey, "More Grads Finding Part-Time Work, StatsCan Finds," *Toronto Star*, 14 March 1998.

37 Cited in Lowe, *The Quality of Work*, 68, 92, 94, 110; Livingstone, *The Education-Jobs Gap*, chapter 3.

38 Livingstone, "Living in the Credential Gap," 226.

39 Livingstone, *The Education-Jobs Gap*, cited, 106.

40 "Lives on Hold:" Youth Job Crisis – A Special Report," *Toronto Star*, 6 December 1997, SS2.

41 Lowe, "Computers in the Workplace," 29–36.

42 Livingstone, *The Education-Jobs Gap*, 48–9.

43 Ibid., chapter 3; Lowe, *The Quality of Work*, 89–90, 114–15.

44 Lowe, *The Quality of Work*, 172–81.

45 Ibid., 85.

46 McPherson and Shapiro, "Economic Challenges for Liberal Arts Colleges," 47–75; Armstrong and Casement, *The Child and the Machine*.

47 Lipman-Bluman, "The Creative Tension between Liberal Arts and Specialization," 17–25

48 Lowe, *The Quality of Work*, 86.

49 Ibid., 85, 87.

50 Brethour, "High-Tech Skills Keeping Pace with Computer Job Boom," *Globe and Mail*, 11 June 1998. See also Stanford, "Why the Computer E-Emperor Has No Clothes," *Globe and Mail*, 23 March 2000.

51 Tuck and Bourette, "Nortel Cuts, Investors Run," *Globe and Mail*, 16 February 2001; Theobald, "Jobs, Output Drop," *Toronto Star*, 31 March 2001; Hamilton, "Nortel Cuts 20,000 More Jobs," *Toronto Star*, 3 October 2001.

52 The economist cited is Michael Skolnik, in Lewington, "Ontario Universities Weary of Tory High-Tech Plan," *Globe and Mail*, 6 June 1998. For a detailed discussion of the limits of manpower planning, including the engineering case cited in the text, see Axelrod, *Scholars and Dollars*, 176–7.

53 Campbell, "Hot New Jobs: Teachers, Nurses and Bureaucrats," *Globe and Mail*, 23 January 1999, A1.

54 See Clark, "Search for Success," 174–9; Crozier and Grassick, "'I Love My B.A,' 19–26; Schaffer, *The Ultimate Job Guide for Young Canadians*; and Munschauer, *Jobs for English Majors and Other Smart People* (Peterson's Guides; there are similar books on other disciplines in this series).

CHAPTER 4

1 Cameron, *More Than an Academic Question*, part 1. See also Jones, *Higher Education in Canada*.

2 Axelrod, *Scholars and Dollars*.

3 Axelrod, "Higher Education in Canada and the United States," 168.

4 Norrie and Owram, *A History of the Canadian Economy.*

5 Cohen, "Trading Away the Public System," 123–41.

6 Krahn and Lowe, *Work, Industry, and Canadian Society.*

7 Shumar, *College for Sale*; Hart and Livingstone, "The 'Crisis' of Confidence in Schools and the Neoconservative Agenda," 1–19; Jane Kelsey, cited in Smith, "Economic Fundamentalism, Globalization and the Public Remains of Education," 93–117.

8 Ontario Jobs and Investment Board, *A Road Map to Prosperity,* 17.

9 Alexander, "The Changing Face of Accountability," 427.

10 Slaughter, "National Higher Education Policies in a Global Economy," 46.

11 Government contributions to "not-for-profit heritage institutions" declined from 77 per cent of operating revenues in 1991 to 65 per cent in 1995–96. See Luffman, "The Gift and the Giver, 1–8. For a critical view of eroding government support for cultural institutions, see Scott, "Why I Quit," *Globe and Mail,* 4 December 2000. The author resigned as chief executive officer of the Ontario Arts Council.

12 For an elaboration of some of these themes, see Saul, *The Unconscious Civilization.*

13 Canadian Association of University Teachers, *Not in the Public Interest*; quotation from page 5.

14 Canadian Association of University Teachers, "The Canada Research Chairs."

15 Prichard, *Federal Support for Higher Education and Research in Canada,* 37–8.

16 Cited in Bentley, "Humanities for Humanity's Sake," 17.

17 Angenot, "The Misery of Quebec's Universities."

18 Barnetson and Boberg, "Resource Allocation and Public Policy in Alberta's Postsecondary System," 57–86; quotation, 64.

19 The number of part-time faculty in Canada grew by 6 per cent

between 1992/93 to 1997/98, while that of full-time faculty fell
by 2.3 per cent. The increase was especially high in Atlantic
Canada and western Canada. See Statistics Canada, "Part-Time
University Faculty." See also Tudiver, *Universities for Sale*,
75–7.

20 Bruneau, "Shall We Perform, or Shall We Be Free?" 161–80.
See also Barnetson and Boberg, "Resource Allocation and
Public Policy," 75–7.

21 Dowsett Johnston, "A Map to Prosperity," 53.

22 Gilbert, "Performance Indicators for Universities," 20–1.

23 Grosjean, et al., *Measuring the Unmeasurable*, part v, 3.

24 Ibid., part iv, 4.

25 Ibid., part ii, 10; Polster and Newson, "Don't Count Your
Blessings," 175.

26 See *Maclean's*, "The Universities 2000," 52–110. Of course
many of the criticisms of performance indicators could be
made (and have been) of the *Maclean's* ranking system itself,
which compares Canadian universities on the basis of selected
quantified measurements. See Page, "Rankings of Canadian
Universities," 452–7.

27 Burke and Modarresi, "To Keep or Not to Keep Performance
Funding," 432.

28 Groulx, "Marc Renaud: Restoring the Value of Humanities
Research," 14–15.

29 Calamai, "'Screening' of Grants Worries Researchers," *Toronto
Star*, 3 July 2001. For a discussion of the early history of
strategic grants, see Fisher, *The Social Sciences in Canada*.

30 Calamai, "Profit Spin-Off Plan Is Panned," *Toronto Star*, 10
March 2000.

31 Tudiver, *Universities for Sale*, 152.

32 Networks of Centres of Excellence, Policies and Guidelines,
Networks of Centres of Excellence, Phase ii, December 1995,
cited in Tudiver, *Universities for Sale*, 152.

33 Networks of Centres of Excellence, "NCE Partners," 2000. See

also Polster, "Dismantling the Liberal University," 106–21.

34 Kornberg, "Invention Is the Mother of Necessity," *Globe and Mail*, 4 November 2000, A15. A similar case is made by the biochemist Hans Kornberg, "Balancing Pure and Applied Research," 87–108.

35 Cole, "Ivy-League Hustle," 35–44.

36 Clark, "Academia in the Service of Industry," 73.

37 Press and Washburn, "The Kept University," 42.

38 Ibid., 40. See also Blumenstyk, "Berkeley Pact with a Swiss Company Takes Technology Transfer to a New Level." For examples of similar cases, see Axelrod, "Service or Captivity?" 45–68, and Myeroff, "Science and the Public Trust," 69–85. See also Etzkowitz and Kemelgor, "The Role of Research Centres in the Collectivisation of Academic Science," 271–88.

39 Blumenstyk, "Scientific Journals Rarely Disclose Authors' Potential Conflicts, Study Finds."

40 Krimsky et al., "Financial Interests of Authors in Scientific Journals," 395–410. Michael McCarthy, an editor at the British medical journal *The Lancet*, noted that financial links of authors to companies sponsoring research are common. He "often can't find anyone who doesn't have a financial interest in a drug or therapy the journal would like to review" (Press and Washburn, "The Kept University," 42–3).

41 McIlroy, "Drug Research Walks Thin Line," *Globe and Mail*, 1 January 2001, A5.

42 There are a number of articles on the Olivieri case. She provides her own account in Nancy Olivieri, "When Money and Truth Collide," in *The Corporate Campus*, ed. Turk, 53–62.

43 Canadian Medical Association, "Look, No Strings," 733. See also Davidoff et al., "Sponsorship, Authorship and Accountability," 786.

44 A footnote to this saga: in 1998, Robert Prichard, then president of the University of Toronto, had lobbied the federal government on behalf of Apotex Inc. for a "30-day extension to a

review of drug-patent protection regulations." New federal
directives had evidently threatened to make it "financially
impossible for Apotex to fulfill its $20 million donation toward
the University's new centre for Cellular and Biomolecular
Research." Recognizing the inappropriateness of his actions,
Prichard apologized to the university's executive committee. See
Foss and Luksic, "Lobbying for Donor Drug Firm a Mistake,
U of T Head Admits," *Globe and Mail*, 16 September 1999, A8.

45 See Warde, "Conflicts of Interest on the Campus."

46 Bok, *Beyond the Ivory Tower*, 142.

47 Arthurs, Blais, and Thompson, *Integrity in Scholarship*, 12.

48 Monahan, "The Fabrikant Case at Concordia University," 146.

49 Clark, "Academia in the Service of Industry," 74.

50 Canadian Association of University Teachers, "Information
    Paper: University/Business Relationships in Research and
    Development." See also a series of recommendations proposed
    by a number of health researchers in Canada: Steven Lewis,
    Patricia Baird, Robert G. Evans, William S. Ghali, Charles J.
    Wright, Elaine Gibson, Françoise Baylis, "Dancing with the
    Porcupine: Rules for Governing the University-Industry Rela-
    tionship," 783.

51 Ontario Confederation of University Faculty Associations,
    "Briefing Note, Bill 132: Ministry of Training, Colleges and
    Universities Statute Law Amendment Act 2000," 23 October
    2000; Ontario Ministry of Training, Colleges and Universities,
    "News Release: New Legislation Will Offer More Choice to
    Postsecondary Students."

52 Ontario, Ministry of Finance, "News Release: Canada's Newest
    University to Meet the Demand for Market-Driven Degree Pro-
    grams – Province to Invest $60 Million in Ontario Institute of
    Technology." The institute is scheduled to open in 2003.

53 Ontario Council on University Affairs, "A Policy Recommen-
    dation on Freestanding, Secular, Degree-Granting Institutions
    in Ontario," 263.

54 Leatherman, "U of Phoenix's Faculty Members Insist They
   Offer High-Quality Education"; Seligo, "U of Phoenix Picks
   New Jersey for Its First Foray in Eastern U.S."; Winston,
   "For-Profit Higher Education," 13–19; "Phoenix Campus Rises
   in B.C.," *The Province*, 14 January 1999, A37.

55 Ryan, "Higher Education as a Business," 124.

56 Howard, "An Ivory Tower's Radical Blueprint," *Globe and
   Mail*, 11 January 1999, A1, A7. See also Sokoloff, "Ontario
   May Get Private Universities," *National Post*, 31 July 2001, A4.

57 See Cohen, "Trading Away the Public System," 123–41; quotation from 132.

58 Altbach, "Why Higher Education Is Not a Global Commodity."

59 Ralph Klein, the premier of Alberta, called for private postsecondary institutions to be given degree-granting status in order
   to "offset looming shortages of some professionals in the
   health and educational sectors." See Olsen, "Broader Role Seen
   for Private Schools," *Calgary Herald*, 19 February 2001.

60 Trow, "The Exceptionalism of American Higher Education,"
   159.

61 Cited in *CAUT Bulletin*, "Ontario Universities Continue to
   Lose Ground," June 2000, 4.

62 Canadian Association of University Teachers, "Government
   Cuts to Post-secondary Education," 127; "University Research
   Libraries Continue to Slide in Rankings," CUFA/BC wire
   <http://www.cufa.bc.ca.> 4 October 1999.

63 Tudiver, *Universities for Sale*, 83–137. For an alternative, more
   critical view of the role of unions in Canadian universities, see
   Cameron, *More Than an Academic Question*, 343–89.

64 This is confirmed in Grayson, *Follow-Up Survey of Strike
   Impact*.

65 Bouchard and Zaro, "University Education: Recent Trends
   in Participation, Accessibility and Returns."

66 Gray, "Arts Tuition Increases Levelling Off, Statistics Reveal";
   Statistics Canada, "University Tuition Fees."

67 Rushowy, "Tuition Deters Poor, Study Finds," *Toronto Star*,
    23 March 2000, A8.
68 Finance Canada, "Helping Manage Student Debt"; Finnie,
    "Measuring the Load," 19.
69 Fine, "Medical School Fees Exclude Poor," *Globe and Mail*,
    4 April 2001. The survey of 330 first-year students did not
    control for inflation.
70 Rushowy, "Liberal Arts Suffering, Faculty Organization Says,"
    Toronto Star, 8 March 2000, A2; Grosjean et al., *Measuring the
    Unmeasurable*, part III, 3–4.
71 Statistics Canada, "University Degrees Granted by Field of
    Study, by Sex." These figures are not terribly well refined.
    Many of those categorized as humanities and social sciences
    students may well have specialties in areas normally outside the
    liberal arts field. At York University, for example, large num-
    bers of arts students are specializing in programs called "Busi-
    ness and Society" and "Information Technology."
72 Sorum, "Vortex, Clouds and Tongue," 252. Note that Canadi-
    an figures are for universities only while the American figures
    include colleges and universities.
73 Guy Neave, cited in Slaughter and Leslie, *Academic
    Capitalism*, 40.

CHAPTER 5

1 Gibson, *To Serve and Yet Be Free*, 110; Eells, "Criticisms of
   Higher Education, 398–9; Bercuson, Bothwell, and Granatstein, *The Great Brain Robbery* and *Petrified Campus*.
2 For additional examples of such writing, see Axelrod,
   "Romancing the Past," 61–74.
3 See McLaren, *Our Own Master Race*.
4 Anglin and Meng, "Evidence on Grades and Grade Inflation
   at Ontario's Universities," 361–8.
5 *Toronto Star*, 30 October 1996.
6 Bercuson, Bothwell, and Granatstein, *Petrified Campus*, 60.

7   Potelli and Vibert, "Dare We Criticize Common Educational Standards?" 69–79; Toplak and Wiener, "A Critical Analysis of Grade 3 Testing in Ontario," 65–85.

8   For a critical review of one province's experience with curriculum reform, see Gidney, *From Hope to Harris*. See also Emberley and Newell, *Bankrupt Education*.

9   Sax et al., *The American Freshman*; Astin, *What Matters in College?* Levine and Cureton, *When Hope and Fear Collide*; Gilbert et al., *From Best Intentions to Best Practices*, chapter 4.

10 Gomme, Hall, and Murphy, "In the Shadow of the Tower," 18–35.

11 Gilbert et al., *From Best Intentions to Best Practices*, 45.

12 Pascarella and Terenzini, *How College Affects Students*, 560.

13 Kingwell, *The World We Want*, 161.

14 Lowman, "Professors as Performers and Motivators," 137–41.

15 Charles Schroeder, cited in Sorum "Vortex, Clouds and Tongue," 254.

16 Davis and Schroeder. "New Students in Liberal Arts Colleges," 164, 166.

17 Johnson, Johnson, and Smith, "Constructive Controversy," 28–37.

18 Weaver, *Liberal Education*, cited on 54.

19 Ibid., 57.

20 Useem, *Liberal Education and the Corporation*, 69.

21 Mierson, with Parikah, "Stories from the Field," 23.

22 Matson and Matson, "Changing Times in Higher Education," 13–24; Stanton, "Liberal Arts, Experiential Learning and Public Service," 55–68; Simon, Dippo, and Schenke, *Learning Work*; Useem, *Liberal Education and the Corporation*, 80–2.

23 Dewey, *Experience and Education*, 20, 36.

24 Ryan, *Liberal Anxieties and Liberal Education*, 124.

25 Haggart, "Picture a Privately Funded, Classical Education on a Public Campus," 1–2.

26 Mendelsohn, "Liberal Arts College of Concordia University, Montreal," 38.

27 Good, "The Search for Synthesis," 7–23.

28 Schofield, "Back to School Online," 25.

29 Cited in the *Vancouver Sun*, 13 November 1998.

30 Clark, "The Problem of Complexity in Modern Higher Education," 276–7.

31 *Teaching at an Internet Distance*, 23–9.

32 *Globe and Mail*, 20 January 2001.

33 *Teaching at an Internet Distance*, 8–9.

34 Council of Ontario Universities, *A Time to Sow*, 4.

35 Noble, "Digital Diploma Mills," part 1, 12–16.

36 Blumenstyk, "The Marketing Intensifies in Distance Learning."

37 Alliance for Childhood, *Fool's Gold*. The report cites Cuban, *The Classroom Use of Technology since 1920*.

38 *Teaching at an Internet Distance*, 3, 29.

39 Neal, "Using Technology in Teaching."

40 Cited in Axelrod, "Romancing the Past," 69.

41 Psychosocial Paediatrics Committee, Canadian Paediatric Society, "Children and the Media," 350. For an informed discussion of this literature, see Wright, *Hip and Trivial*, chapter 4.

42 Armstrong and Casement, *The Child and the Machine*.

43 Statistics Canada, "Average Hours Per Week of Television Viewing, Fall 1998."

44 Roosmalen and Krahn, "Boundaries of Youth," 3–39.

45 Bethune and Turbide, "The Kidlit Boom," cited in Wright, *Hip and Trivial*, 120–1.

46 A comprehensive (1991) study of Canadian reading habits found that Canadians over 65 read the most – 33.9 books annually – followed by 15 to 19 year olds, who read an average of 25.4 books per year. (Graves and Dugas, *Reading in Canada 1991*, cited in Wright, *Hip and Trivial*, 131).

47 Niedzviecki, *We Want Some Too*, 20–6.

CONCLUSION

1 Clark, "The Problem of Complexity in Modern Higher Education," 268.

2 Barnett, *Realizing the University in an Age of Supercomplexity*, 22, 43, 166.

3 Readings, *The University in Ruins*.

Further Reading on Liberal Education and the University

Anderson, Charles W. *Prescribing the Life of the Mind: An Essay on the Purpose of the University, the Aims of Liberal Education, the Competence of Citizens, and the Cultivation of Practical Reason.* Madison, Wis.: University of Wisconsin Press, 1993

Barnett, Ronald. *Realizing the University in an Age of Supercomplexity.* Buckingham, Eng.: Society for Research in Higher Education and the Open University, 2000

Bloom, Allan. *The Closing of the American Mind.* New York: Simon and Schuster, 1987

Carnochan, W.B. *The Battleground of the Curriculum: Liberal Education and the American Experience.* Stanford: Stanford University Press, 1993

Emberley, Peter. *Zero Tolerance: Hot Button Politics in Canada's Universities.* Toronto: Penguin Books, 1996

Kimball, Bruce A. *Orators and Philosophers: A History of the Idea of Liberal Education.* New York: College Entrance Examination Board, 1995

Levine, Lawrence W. *The Opening of the American Mind: Canons, Culture and History.* Boston: Beacon Press, 1996

Newman, John Henry. *The Idea of a University*, ed. Frank M. Turner. New Haven: Yale University Press, 1996

Nussbaum, Martha C. *Cultivating Humanity: A Classical Defense of Reform in Liberal Education.* Harvard University: Cahners 1997

Pelikan, Jaroslav. *The Idea of a University: A Reeaxamination.* New Haven: Yale University Press, 1992

Readings, Bill. *The University in Ruins.* Cambridge, Mass.: Harvard University Press, 1996

Rothblatt, Sheldon. "The Limbs of Osiris: Liberal Education in the English-Speaking World." In *The European and American University since 1800: Historical and Sociological Essays*, ed. Sheldon Rothblatt and Björn Wittrock, Cambridge: Cambridge University Press, 1993

Ryan, Ian. *Liberal Anxieties and Liberal Education.* New York: Hill and Wang, 1998

Shorris, Earl. *Riches for the Poor: The Clemente Course in the Humanities.* New York: W.W. Norton, 2000

Slaughter, Sheila, and Larry L. Leslie. *Academic Capitalism: Politics, Policies and the Entrepreneurial University.* Baltimore: Johns Hopkins University Press, 1997

Weaver, Frederick Stirton. *Liberal Education: Critical Essays on Professions, Pedagogy and Structure.* New York: Teachers College, Columbia University, 1991

Whitehead, Alfred North. *The Aims of Education and Other Essays.* New York: Macmillan, 1929

Bibliography

Acharya, Madhavi. "The University Won't Beat College Diploma: Poll." *Toronto Star*, 15 July 1998

Alexander, F. King. "The Changing Face of Accountability: Monitoring and Assessing Institutional Performance in Higher Education." *Journal of Higher Education* 71, no. 4 (2000): 411–31

Allard, Paul, Paul Bates, Everett Anstey, and Kevin Bannis. "Hi-Tech CEOs Say Value of Liberal Arts Is Increasing." Text of CEO statement. Toronto: New Paradigm Learning Corporation, c. 7 April 2000

Allen, Robert C. "The Employability of University Graduates in the Humanities, Social Sciences, and Education: Recent Statistical Evidence." Discussion paper 98–15, Department of Economics, University of British Columbia, 1998

Alliance for Childhood. *Fool's Gold: A Critical Look at Computers and Childhood,* <www.allianceforchildhood.htm> 2000

Alphonso, Caroline. "School of Hard Knocks Mixes Plato, Poverty." *Globe and Mail*, 6 January 2001

Altbach, Philip G."Why Higher Education Is Not a Global Commodity." *Chronicle of Higher Education*, 11 May 2001

American Association for the Advancement of Science. *The Liberal
Art of Science: Agenda for Action*. Washington: American Association for the Advancement of Science, 1993

Anderson, Charles W. *Prescribing the Life of the Mind: An Essay on
the Purpose of the University, the Aims of Liberal Education, the
Competence of Citizens, and the Cultivation of Practical Reason*.
Madison, Wis.: University of Wisconsin Press, 1993

Angenot, Marc. "The Misery of Quebec's Universities." *Cité Libre*,
27, no. 3 (1999): 67–72

Anglin, Paul M, and Ronald Meng. "Evidence on Grades and
Grade Inflation at Ontario's Universities." *Canadian Public Policy* 26, no. 3 (2000): 361–8

Anisef, Paul, and Paul Axelrod. "Universities, Graduates and the
Marketplace: Canadian Trends and Prospects." In *Transitions:
Schooling and Employment in Canada*, ed. Anisef and Axelrod,
103–14. Toronto: Thompson Educational Publishers, 1993

Armstrong, Alison, and Charles Casement. *The Child and the
Machine: Why Computers Put Our Children's Education at Risk*.
Toronto: Key Porter Books, 1998

Arthurs, H.W., Roger A. Blais, and Jon Thompson. *Integrity in
Scholarship: A Report to Concordia University*. Montreal: Concordia University, 1994

Association of American Colleges. *Liberal Learning and the Arts
and Science Majors*, vol. 2: *Reports from the Fields*. Washington:
Association of American Colleges, 1991

Astin, Alexander W. *What Matters in College? Four Critical Years
Revisited*. San Francisco: Jossey Bass, 1992

Axelrod, Paul. "Higher Education in Canada and the United States:
Exploring the Roots of Difference." *Historical Studies in
Education* 7, no. 1 (1995): 141–75

– *Making a Middle Class: Student Life in English Canada during
the Thirties*. Montreal and Kingston: McGill-Queen's University
Press, 1990

- "Romancing the Past: Nostalgic Conservatism, *The Great Brain Robbery*, and the History of Education." In *Historical Perspectives on Educational Policy in Canada: Issues, Debates and Case Studies*, ed. Eric W. Ricker and B. Anne Wood, 61–74. Toronto: Canadian Scholars Press, 1995

- *Scholars and Dollars: Politics, Economics and the Universities of Ontario, 1945– 1980*. Toronto: University of Toronto Press, 1982

- "Service or Captivity? Business-University Relations in the Twentieth Century." In *University in Crisis: A Medieval Institution in the Twenty-First Century*, ed. William Neilson and Chad Gaffield, 45–68. Montreal: Institute for Research on Public Policy, 1986

Axelrod, Paul, Paul Anisef, and Zeng Lin. "Against All Odds? The Enduring Value of Liberal Education in Universities, the Professions, and the Labour Market." *Canadian Journal of Higher Education* 31, no. 2, (2001): 47–77

Barnetson, Bob, and Alice Boberg. "Resource Allocation and Public Policy in Alberta's Postsecondary System." *Canadian Journal of Higher Education* 30, no. 2 (2000): 57–86

Barnett, Ronald, *Realizing the University in an Age of Supercomplexity*. Buckingham, Eng.: Society for Research in Higher Education and the Open University, 2000

Bentley, David. "Humanities for Humanity's Sake." *University Affairs*, 20 April 2000

Bercuson, David, Robert Bothwell, and J.L. Granatstein. *The Great Brain Robbery: Canada's Universities on the Road to Ruin*. Toronto: McClelland and Stewart, 1984

- *Petrified Campus: The Crisis in Canada's Universities*. Toronto: Random House of Canada, 1997

Bethune, Brian, and Diane Turbide. "The Kidlit Boom." *Maclean's*, 11 December 1995

Bledstein, Burton. *The Culture of Professionalism: The Middle Class and the Development of Higher Education in America*. New York: W.W. Norton, 1976

Bloom, Allan. *The Closing of the American Mind*. New York: Simon and Schuster, 1987

Blumenstyk, Goldie. "Berkeley Pact with a Swiss Company Takes Technology Transfer to a New Level." *Chronicle of Higher Education*, 11 December 1998

– "The Marketing Intensifies in Distance Learning." *Chronicle of Higher Education*, 5 April 1999

– "Scientific Journals Rarely Disclose Authors' Potential Conflicts, Study Finds." *Chronicle of Higher Education*, 28 January 1999

Bok, Derek C. *Beyond the Ivory Tower: Social Responsibilities of the Modern University*. Cambridge, Mass.: Harvard University, 1982

Bond, Adrienne. "The Arts That Liberate." In *Pioneers and Pallbearers: Perspectives on Liberal Education*, ed. JoAnna M. Watson and Rex P. Stevens, 127–45. Macon, Ga.: Mercer University, 1982

Bouchard, Brigitte, and John Zaro. "University Education: Recent Trends in Participation, Accessibility and Returns." *Education Quarterly Review* 6, no. 4 (2000). "Article Highlights." <http://www.statcan.ca/english/indepth/81003feature/eq2000_v06 n4_sum_a02_hi.htm>

Brethour, Patrick. "High-Tech Skills Keeping Pace with Computer Job Boom." *Globe and Mail*, 11 June 1998

Brubacher, John S., and Willis Rudy. *Higher Education in Transition: A History of American Colleges and Universities, 1636–1976*. New York: Harper and Rowe, 1976

Bruneau, William. "Shall We Perform, or Shall We Be Free?" In *The Corporate Campus: Commercialization and the Dangers to Canada's Colleges and Universities*, ed. James L. Turk, 161–180. Toronto: James Lorimer, 2000

Burke, Joseph C., and Shahpar Modarresi. "To Keep or Not to Keep Performance Funding." *Journal of Higher Education* 71, no. 4 (2000): 443–53

Calamai, Peter. "Profit Spin-Off Plan Is Panned." *Toronto Star*, 10 March 2000

- "'Screening' of Grants Worries Researchers." *Toronto Star*, 3 July 2001

Cameron, David M. *More Than an Academic Question: Universities, Government, and Public Policy in Canada*. Halifax: Institute for Research on Public Policy, 1991

Campbell, Murray. "Hot New Jobs: Teachers, Nurses and Bureaucrats." *Globe and Mail*, 23 January 1999

Canadian Association of University Teachers. "The Canada Research Chairs: Not in the Public Interest." *Commentary* 2, no. 1 (2000). <http://www.caut.ca/English/Publications/Commentary/Vol2No1_Chairs.htm>

- *Bulletin Online* 44, no. 9 (1997)

- "Government Cuts to Post-secondary Education." In *Missing Pieces: An Alternative Guide to Canadian Post-Secondary Education*, ed. Denise Doherty-Delorme and Erika Shaker. Ottawa: Canadian Centre for Policy Alternatives, 1999

- "Information Paper: University/Business Relationships in Research and Development: A Guide for Universities and Researchers," approved in 1987. <http://www.caut.ca/English/CAUTframe.html>

- *Not in the Public Interest: University Finance in Canada, 1972–1998*. Ottawa: Canadian Association of University Teachers, 2000

- "Ontario Universities Continue to Lose Ground." CAUT *Bulletin*, June 2000, 4

Canadian Conference of the Arts Web site <www.culturenet.ca/cca/artfacts.htm> 2000

Canadian Education Statistics Council. *A Statistical Portrait of Education at the University Level*. Ottawa: Statistics Canada, 1996

Canadian Medical Association. "Look, No Strings: Publishing Industry-Funded Research." *Canadian Medical Association Journal* 165, no. 5 (2001): 733

Carey, Elaine. "More Grads Finding Part-Time Work, StatsCan Finds." *Toronto Star,* 14 March 1998

Carnochan, W.B. *The Battleground of the Curriculum: Liberal Education and the American Experience.* Stanford: Stanford University Press, 1993

Clark, Burton. "The Problem of Complexity in Modern Higher Education." In *The European and American University since 1800: Historical and Sociological Essays,* ed. Sheldon Rothblatt and Bjorn Wittrock, 276–97. Cambridge: Cambridge University Press, 1993

Clark, E. Ann. "Academia in the Service of Industry: The Ag Biotech Model." In *The Corporate Campus: Commercialization and the Dangers to Canada's Colleges and Universities,* ed. James L. Turk, 69–86. Toronto: James Lorimer, 2000

Clark, Warren. "Search for Success: Finding Work after Graduation." In *Canadian Social Trends,* vol. 3, 174–9. Toronto: Thompson Educational Publishers, 2000

Cohen, Marjorie Griffin. "Trading Away the Public System: The WTO and Post-secondary Education." In *The Corporate Campus: Commercialization and the Dangers to Canada's Colleges and Universities,* ed. James L. Turk, 123–41. Toronto: James Lorimer, 2000

Cole, Trevor. "Ivy-League Hustle." *Globe and Mail Report on Business Magazine,* June, 1998, 35–44

Collins, Randall. *The Credential Society: An Historical Sociology of Education and Stratification.* New York: Academic Press, 1979

Conference Board of Canada. "Employability Skills 2000+." <www.conferenceboard.ca/nbec> May 2000

Council of Ontario Universities. "Highlights from the 1999–2000 Ontario University Graduate Survey." Toronto: Council of Ontario Universities, April 2000

– *A Time to Sow: Report from the Task Force on Learning Technologies.* Toronto: Council of Ontario Universities, March 2000

"Course Teaches Humanities for the Poor." *Vancouver Sun,* 29 February 2000

Cromie, Mary, and Rochelle Handelman. "Consumption and Participation in the Culture Sector." *Focus on Culture* (Statistics
Canada Publication), 11. no. 3 (1999): 1–5

Crozier, Sharon D., and Patrick Grassick. "'I Love My BA,' The
Employment Experience of Successful Bachelor of Arts Graduates." *Guidance Counselling* 11. no. 2 (1996): 19–26

Cuban, Larry. *The Classroom Use of Technology since 1920.* New
York: Teachers College Press, 1986

Das, Satya. "New Economy Craves Graduates with Arts Degrees,
Congress Told." *Edmonton Journal,* 27 May 2000

Davidoff, Frank, et al. "Sponsorship, Authorship and Accountability." *Canadian Medical Association Journal* 165, no. 6 (2001): 786

Davis, Marjorie T., and Charles C. Schroeder. "New Students in
Liberal Arts Colleges: Threat or Challenge?" In *Pioneers and
Pallbearers: Perspectives on Liberal Education,* ed. JoAnna M.
Watson and Rex P. Stevens, 147–68. Macon, Ga.: Mercer Univer-
sity Press, 1982

Dewey, John. *Experience and Education.* New York: Macmillan,
[1938] 1963

Domonkos, Leslie S. "History of Higher Education." In *International Encyclopedia of Higher Education,* 1–22. San Francisco:
Jossey Bass, 1977

Dowsett Johnston, Ann. "A Map to Prosperity." *Maclean's,*
17 April 2000, 53

Eells, Walter Crosby. "Criticisms of Higher Education: Picturesque
Exaggerations Found in Current Writings." *Journal of Higher
Education* 50 (April 1934): 398–9

Emberley, Peter C. *Zero Tolerance: Hot Button Politics in Canada's
Universities.* Toronto: Penguin Books, 1996

Emberley, Peter, and Waller Newell. *Bankrupt Education: The
Decline of Liberal Education in Canada.* Toronto: University of
Toronto Press, 1994

Etzkowitz, Henry, and Carol Kemelgor. "The Role of Research
Centres in the Collectivisation of Academic Science." *Minerva* 36
(1998): 271–88

"Evolution of Engineering Education in Canada: New Challenges for Canadian Universities." *Engineering Issues* 8 (December 1999): 1–2

Fekete, John. *Moral Panic: Biopolitics Rising*. Montreal: Robert Davies, 1994

Finance Canada. "Helping Manage Student Debt." February 1998. <http://www.fin.gc.ca/budget98/pamphe/studpae.htm>

Fine, Sean. "Medical School Fees Exclude Poor." *Globe and Mail*, 4 April 2001

Finnie, Ross. "Measuring the Load, Easing the Burden." *Commentary* (C.D. Howe Institute), November 2001, 1–32

Fisher, Donald. *The Social Sciences in Canada: Fifty Years of National Activity by the Social Science Federation of Canada*. Waterloo: Wilfrid Laurier Press, 1991

Foss, Krista, and Nicola Luksic. "Lobbying for Donor Drug Firm a Mistake, U of T Head Admits." *Globe and Mail*, 16 September 1999

Francis, Diane. "Universities Grabbing Too Big a Slice of the Education Pie." *Financial Post*, 23 September 1998

Freedman, James O. *Idealism and Liberal Education*. Ann Arbor: University of Michigan Press, 1996

Fulford, Robert. "Canadian Science Writing Undernourished, Inferior." *Globe and Mail*, 19 August 1998

Galt, Virginia. "More Prefer College to University: Poll." *Globe and Mail*, 22 June 1999

Garrison, Nicholas. "Business Loves the BA." NOW magazine, 9–15 March 2000, 30, 33

Gibson, Frederick W. *To Serve and Yet Be Free: Queen's University*. Vol. 2. Montreal and Kingston: McGill-Queen's University Press, 1983

Gidney, R.D. *From Hope to Harris: The Reshaping of Ontario's Schools*. Toronto: University of Toronto Press, 1998

Gidney, R.D., and W.P.J. Millar. *Professional Gentlemen: The Professions in Nineteenth-Century Ontario*. Toronto: University of Toronto Press, 1994

Gilbert, Sid. "Performance Indicators for Universities: Ogres or
   Opportunities." OCUFA *Forum*, Spring 1999, 20–1

Gilbert, Sid, Judy Chapman, Peter Dietsche, Paul Grayson, and
   John N. Gardner. *From Best Intentions to Best Practices: The
   First-Year Experience in Canadian Postsecondary Education.*
   Columbia, S.C.: University of South Carolina, 1997

Godsoe, P.C. "Universities Must Excel Despite Less Funding."
   Canadian Speeches 10, no. 1 (1996): 40–5

Gomme, Ian M., Mary P. Hall, and Terry J. Murphy. "In the Shadow of the Tower: The View of the Undergraduate Experience."
   Canadian Journal of Higher Education 23, no. 3 (1993): 18–35

Good, Sinclair. "The Search for Synthesis: Constraints on the Development of the Humanities in Liberal Science-Based Education."
   Studies in Higher Education 25, no. 1 (2000): 7–23

Granatstein, J.L *Who Killed Canadian History?* Toronto:
   HarperCollins, 1998

Graves, Frank L., and Timothy Dugas. *Reading in Canada, 1991.*
   Ottawa: Ekos Research Associates, 1991

Gray, Jeff. "Arts Tuition Increases Levelling Off, Statistics Reveal."
   Globe and Mail, 28 August 2001

Grayson, J. Paul. *Experiences of York Graduates – Two Years
   Later.* Toronto: York University, Institute for Social Research,
   1998

– *Follow-Up Survey of Strike Impact.* Toronto: York University,
   Institute for Social Research, 1997

Grosjean, G., J. Atkinson-Grosjean, K. Rubenson, and D. Fisher.
   *Measuring the Unmeasurable: Paradoxes of Accountability and
   the Impacts of Performance Indicators on Liberal Education in
   Canada.* Ottawa: Humanities and Social Science Federation of
   Canada, 2000.
   <wysiwyg://68/http://www.hssfc.ca/ResearchProj/PerfInd/FinalRe-
   portEng.html>

Groulx, Michel. "Marc Renaud: Restoring the Value of Humanities
   Research." *University Affairs*, February 1998, 14–15

Guppy, Neil, and Scott Davies. *Education in Canada: Recent*

Trends and Future Challenges. Ottawa: Ministry of Industry, 1998

Haggart, Blayne. "Picture a Privately Funded, Classical Education on a Public Campus." *Catholic New Times*, 17 May 1998, 1–2

Hamilton, Tyler. "Nortel Cuts 20,000 More Jobs." *Toronto Star*, 3 October 2001

Harris, Robin S. *A History of Higher Education in Canada, 1663–1960*. Toronto: University of Toronto Press, 1976

Hart, Douglas, and D.W. Livingstone. "The 'Crisis' of Confidence in Schools and the Neoconservative Agenda: Diverging Opinions of Corporate Executives and the General Public." *Alberta Journal of Educational Research* 44, no. 1 (1998): 1–19

Hersh, Richard H. "Intentions and Perceptions: A National Survey of Public Attitudes towards Liberal Arts Education." *Change*, March/April, 1997, 16–23

Horn, Michiel. *Academic Freedom in Canada: A History*. Toronto: University of Toronto Press, 1999

Howard, Ross. "An Ivory Tower's Radical Blueprint." *Globe and Mail*, 11 January 1999

Howes, Carol. "Ethics as More Than Just a Course," *National Post*, 28 October 2000

Human Resources Development Canada. Applied Research *Bulletin*. Special edition, Summer 2001

Hutchins, Robert M. *The Higher Learning in America*. New Haven, Conn.: Yale University Press, 1936

Institute for Higher Education Policy. *Reaping the Benefits: Defining the Public and Private Value of Going to College*. Washington, D.C.: Institute for Higher Education Policy, March 1998

Jansen, Theo and Ruud van der Veen. "Adult Education in the Light of the Risk Society." In *The Learning Society: Challenges and Trends*, ed. Richard Edwards Raggat and Nick Small, 122–35. London: Routledge and the Open University, 1996

Jasen, Patricia. "Educating an Elite: A History of the Honour Course System at the University of Toronto." *Ontario History* 81, no. 4 (1989): 269–88

- "'In Pursuit of Human Values (or Laugh When You Say That)':
  The Student Critique of the Arts Curriculum in the 1960s." In
  *Youth, University and Canadian Society: Essays in the Social His-
  tory of Higher Education*, ed. Paul Axelrod and John G. Reid,
  247–71. Montreal and Kingston: McGill-Queen's University
  Press, 1989

Johnson, David W., Roger T. Johnson, and Karl A. Smith. "Constructive Controversy: The Educative Power of Intellectual Conflict." *Change*, January/February, 2000, 28–37

Jones, Glen A., ed. *Higher Education in Canada: Different Systems,
  Different Perspectives*. New York: Garland, 1997

Kett, Joseph. *The Pursuit of Knowledge under Difficulties: From
  Self-Improvement to Adult Education in America, 1750–1990.*
  Stanford: Stanford University Press, 1994

Kimball, Bruce A. *Orators and Philosophers: A History of the Idea
  of Liberal Education.* New York: College Entrance Examination
  Board, 1995

Kingwell, Mark. *The World We Want: Virtue, Vice and the Good
  Citizen.* Toronto: Viking, 2000

Kornberg, Arthur. "Invention Is the Mother of Necessity." *Globe
  and Mail*, 4 November 2000

Kornberg, Hans. "Balancing Pure and Applied Research." In *University in Crisis: A Medieval Institution in the Twenty-First Century*, ed. William Neilson and Chad Gaffield, 87–108. Montreal:
  The Institute for Research on Public Policy, 1986

Krahn, Harvey, and Graham S. Lowe. *1997 Alberta Graduate
  Survey: Labour Market and Educational Experiences of 1994
  University Graduates.* Edmonton: Alberta Advanced Education
  and Career Development, 1998

- "School to Work Transitions and Postmodern Values: What's
  Changing in Canada?" In *From Education to Work: Cross-
  National Perspectives*, ed. Walter R. Heinz, 260–83. Cambridge:
  Cambridge University Press, 1999

- *Work, Industry, and Canadian Society.* 3rd edn. Toronto: ITP
  Nelson, 1999

Krimsky, L.S., P. Stott, L.S. Rothenberg, and G. Kyle. "Financial
Interests of Authors in Scientific Journals: A Pilot Study of Fourteen Publications." *Science and Engineering Ethics* 2,
no. 4 (1996): 395–410

Larson, M.S. *The Rise of Professionalism: A Sociological Analysis.*
Berkeley: University of California Press, 1977

Leamson, Robert N. "Learning without Majoring in It: Tailoring
Multidisciplinary Curricula to Individual Student Interests." *Journal of College Science Teaching* 25, no. 5 (1996): 334–6

Leatherman, Courtney. "U of Phoenix's Faculty Members Insist
They Offer High-Quality Education." *Chronicle of Higher Education*, 12 October 1998

Levine, Arthur, and Jeanette S. Cureton. *When Hope and Fear Collide: A Portrait of Today's College Students.* San Francisco:
Jossey-Bass, 1998

Levine, Lawrence W. *The Opening of the American Mind: Canons,
Culture and History.* Boston: Beacon Press, 1996

Lewington, Jennifer. "Ontario Universities Weary of Tory High-
Tech Plan." *Globe and Mail*, 6 June 1998

Lewis, Steven, Patricia Baird, Robert G. Evans, William S. Ghali,
Charles J. Wright, Elaine Gibson, and Françoise Baylis. "Dancing
with the Porcupine: Rules for Governing the University-Industry
Relationship," *Canadian Medical Association Journal* 165, no. 6
(2001): 783

Lipman-Bluman, Jean. "The Creative Tension between Liberal Arts
and Specialization." *Liberal Education* 81, no. 1 (1995): 17–25

Little, Bruce. "Canadians May Have to Shed Gloom on Jobs
Front." *Globe and Mail*, 21 April 2000

Little, Daniel. "Multiple Goals in Liberal Arts." *Interchange* 29,
no. 3 (1998): 345–50

"Lives on Hold: Youth Job Crisis – A Special Report." *Toronto
Star*, 6 December 1997

Livingstone, D.W. *The Education-Jobs Gap: Underemployment
or Economic Democracy* Toronto: Garamond Press, 1999

– "Living in the Credential Gap: Responses to Underemployment and Overqualification." In *Good Jobs, Bad Jobs, No Jobs: The Transformation of Work in the Twenty-First Century*, ed. Ann Duffy, Daniel Glenday, and Norene Puppo, 217–39. Toronto: Harcourt Brace Canada, 1997

Lowe, Graham S. "Computers in the Workplace." *Perspectives on Labour and Income*, Summer 1997, 29–36

– *The Quality of Work: A People-Centred Agenda*. Toronto: Oxford University Press, 2000

Lowell, Lawrence A., et al. *Final Report of the Commission on Medical Education*. New York: Office of the Director of the Study, 1932

Lowman, Joseph. "Professors as Performers and Motivators." *College Teaching* 42, no. 4 (1994): 137–41

Luffman, Jacqueline. "The Gift and the Giver: Individual Giving to Culture Organizations in Canada." *Focus on Culture* 11, no. 2 (1999): 1–8

McIlroy, Anne. "Drug Research Walks Thin Line." *Globe and Mail*, 1 January 2001

McKillop, A.B. *A Disciplined Intelligence: Critical Inquiry and Canadian Thought in the Victorian Era*. Montreal: McGill-Queen's University Press, 1979

– *Matters of Mind: The University in Ontario, 1791–1951*. Montreal and Kingston: McGill-Queen's University Press, 1994

MacKinnon, Donna Jean. "Arts Degree under the Gun." *Toronto Star*, 27 April 2000

McLaren, Angus. *Our Own Master Race: Eugenics in Canada, 1885–1945*. Toronto: McClelland and Stewart 1990

Maclean's, "The Universities 2000." 20 November 2000, 52–110

McPherson, Michael S., and Morton O. Shapiro. "Economic Challenges for Liberal Arts Colleges." *Daedalus* 128, no. 1 (1999): 47–75

Marchak, Patricia M. *Racism, Sexism, and the University: The Political Science Affair at the University of British Columbia.*

Montreal and Kingston: McGill-Queen's University Press, 1996

Matson, Linda Casey, and Ron Matson. "Changing Times in Higher Education: An Empirical Look at Cooperative Education and Liberal Arts Faculty." *Journal of Cooperative Education* 31, no.1 (1995): 13–24

Mendelsohn, Michele. "Liberal Arts College of Concordia University, Montreal." *In 2 Print* 7 (Spring 1997): 38

Mierson, Sheela, with Anuj A. Parikah. "Stories from the Field: Problem-Based Learning from a Teacher's and a Student's Perspective." *Change*, January/February, 2000

Miller, Richard E. *As If Learning Mattered: Reforming Higher Education* (Ithaca and London: Cornell University Press, 1998)

Mitchell, Thomas N. "From Plato to the Internet." *Change*, March/April, 1999, 17–21

Monahan, Edward J. "The Fabrikant Case at Concordia University: Some Lessons for the Better Management of Universities and Improved Academic Ethics." *Minerva* 33 (1995): 129–48

Munschauer, John. *Jobs for English Majors and Other Smart People*. Princeton, N.J.: Peterson's Guides, 1991

Myeroff, Albert. "Science and the Public Trust: The Need for Reform." In *University in Crisis: A Medieval Institution in the Twenty-First Century*, ed. William Neilson and Chad Gaffield, 69–85. Montreal: Institute for Research on Public Policy, 1986

Neal, Ed. "Using Technology in Teaching: We Need to Exercise Healthy Skepticism." *Chronicle of Higher Education*, 19 June 1998

Nesteruk, Jeffrey. "Business Teaching and Liberal Learning." *Liberal Education* 85, no. 2 (1999): 56–9

Networks of Centres of Excellence. "NCE Partners." <www.nce.gc.ca/en/pubs/99-2000/industypartners_e.htm> 2000

Newman, Cardinal John Henry. *On the Scope and Nature of University Education*. Everyman's Library, no. 723. New York: Dutton 1961

Niedzviecki, Hal. *We Want Some Too: Underground Desire and the*

Reinvention of Mass Culture. Toronto: Penguin Books, 2000

Noble, David F. "Digital Diploma Mills: The Automation of Higher Education," part 1. OCUFA *Forum*, Spring 1998

– *A World without Women: The Christian Clerical Culture of Western Science*. New York: Alfred A. Knopf, 1992

Norrie, Kenneth, and Douglas Owram. *A History of the Canadian Economy*. Toronto: Harcourt Brace Jovanovich, 1991

Nuland, Sherwin B. "The Uncertain Art: The Medical School and the University." *American Scholar* 68, no. 1 (1999): 121–4

Nussbaum, Martha C. *Cultivating Humanity: A Classical Defense of Reform in Liberal Education*. Cambridge, Mass.: Harvard University, Cahners Publishing, 1997

Oblinger, Diana G., and Anne-Lee Verville. *What Business Wants from Higher Education*. American Council on Education. Phoenix, Ariz.: Oryx Press, 1998

O'Heron, Herb. "Different Students, Different Needs." Research files 2, no. 2. Ottawa: Association of Universities and Colleges, November 1997

Olivieri, Nancy. "When Money and Truth Collide." In *The Corporate Campus: Commercialization and the Dangers to Canada's Colleges and Universities*, ed. James L. Turk, 53–62. Toronto: James Lorimer 2000

Olsen, Tom. "Broader Role Seen for Private Schools." *Calgary Herald*, 19 February 2001

Ontario Ministry of Finance. "News Release – Canada's Newest University to Meet the Demand for Market-Driven Degree Programs – Province to Invest $60 Million in Ontario Institute of Technology" <http://www.gov.on.ca/FIN/english/nre-oit.htm> 4 October 2001

Ontario Ministry of Training, Colleges and Universities. "News Release – New Legislation Will Offer More Choice to Postsecondary Students."
<http://www.edu.gov.on.ca/eng/document/nr/00.12/choice.html> 20 December 2000

Ontario Confederation of University Faculty Associations. "Briefing
    Note, Bill 132: Ministry of Training, Colleges and Universities
    Statute Law Amendment Act 2000," 23 October 2000
– "Briefing Note, Targeted Funding," October 2000
Ontario Council on University Affairs. "A Policy Recommendation
    on Freestanding, Secular, Degree-Granting Institutions in
    Ontario." *22nd Annual Report*, 1 April 1995 to 31 August 1996
Ontario Jobs and Investment Board, CEO, David Lindsay. *A Road
    Map to Prosperity: An Economic Plan for Jobs in the Twenty-
    First Century*. Toronto, March, 1999
Orton, James. *The Liberal Education of Women*. New York: A.S.
    Barnes, 1873; reprint, New York: Garland, 1986
Page, Stewart. "Rankings of Canadian Universities, 1997: Statistical
    Contrivance versus Help to Students." *Canadian Journal of Edu-
    cation* 23, no. 4 (1998): 452–7
Paju, Michael. "The Class of '90 Revisited: Report of the 1995
    Follow-Up Survey of 1990 Graduates." *Education Quarterly
    Review* 4, no. 4 (1997): 9–29
Pascarella, Ernest T., and Patrick T. Terenzini. *How College Affects
    Students: Findings and Insights from Twenty Years of Research*.
    San Francisco: Jossey-Bass, 1991
"Phoenix Campus Rises in B.C." *The Province*, 14 January 1999, A37
Plato. *The Laws*. Cited in *Readings in the History of Educational
    Thought*, ed. Alan Cohen and Norman Garner. Toronto: Musson,
    1969
"Plato and Poetry for the Poor." *National Post*, 15 July 2000
Polster, Claire. "Dismantling the Liberal University: The State's
    New Approach to Academic Research." In *The University
    in a Liberal State*, ed. Bob Brecher, Otakar Fleischmann, and
    Jo Halliday, 106–21. Brookfield, Vt.: Ashgate, 1996
Polster, Claire, and Janice Newson. "Don't Count Your Blessings:
    The Social Accomplishments of Performance Indicators." In *Uni-
    versities and Globalization: Critical Perspectives*, ed. Jan Currie
    and Janice Newson, 173–91. Thousand Oaks, Calif.: Sage, 1998

Potelli, John P., and Ann Vibert. "Dare We Criticize Common Educational Standards?" *McGill Journal of Education* 33, no. 1
(1997): 69–79

Press, Eyal, and Jennifer Washburn. "The Kept University." *Atlantic
Monthly*, March 2000

Prichard, J. Robert S. *Federal Support for Higher Education and
Research in Canada: The New Paradigm*. The 2000 Killam Annual Lecture. The Killam Trusts, 2000

Psychosocial Paediatrics Committee, Canadian Paediatric Society.
"Children and the Media." *Paediatrics and Child Health* 4,
no. 5 (1999): 350–4

Readings, Bill. *The University in Ruins*. Cambridge, Mass.: Harvard
University Press, 1996

Roosmalen, Erica Van, and Harvey Krahn. "Boundaries of Youth."
Youth and Society 28, no. 1 (1996): 3–39

Rothblatt, Sheldon."The Limbs of Osiris: Liberal Education in the
English-Speaking World." In *The European and American
University since 1800: Historical and Sociological Essays*,
ed. Sheldon Rothblatt and Bjorn Wittrock, 19–73. Cambridge:
Cambridge University Press, 1993

Rudolph, Frederick. *Curriculum: A History of the American Undergraduate Course of Study since 1636*. San Francisco: Carnegie
Endowment for the Advancement of Learning, 1977

Rushowy, Kristin. "The CEOs Artfully Intervene." *Toronto Star*, 8
April 2000

– "Liberal Arts Suffering, Faculty Organization Says." *Toronto
Star*, 8 March 2000

– "Tuition Deters Poor, Study Finds." *Toronto Star*, 23 March 2000

Ryan, Ian. *Liberal Anxieties and Liberal Education*. New York: Hill
and Wang, 1998

Ryan, Yoni. "Higher Education as a Business: Lessons from the
Corporate World." *Minerva* 39 (2001): 115–35

Saul, John Ralston. *The Unconscious Civilization*. Toronto: Anansi,
1995

Sax, L.J., A.W. Astin, W.S. Korn, and K.M. Mahoney. *The American Freshman: National Norms for Fall, 1998.* Los Angeles: Higher Education Research Institute, 1999

Schafer, Arthur. "Medicine, Morals and Money." *Globe and Mail,* 11 December 1998

Schaffer, Karen. *The Ultimate Job Guide for Young Canadians.* Scarborough, Ont.: Prentice Hall, 1997

Schofield, John. "Back to School Online." *Maclean's,* 6 September 1999

Schrecker, Ellen. *No Ivory Tower: McCarthyism and the Universities.* New York: Oxford University Press, 1986

Schuller, Tom, and Anne Marie Bostyn. "Learners of the Future: Preparing a Policy for the Third Age." In *The Learning Society: Challenges and Trends*, ed. Peter Raggat, Richard Edwards, and Nick Small, 79–95. London: Routledge and the Open University, 1996

Scoffield, Heather. "$500-Million Arts Plan Boosts Internet Culture." *Globe and Mail,* 3 May 2001

Scott, Donna. "Why I Quit." *Globe and Mail,* 4 December 2000

Seligo, Jeffrey. "U of Phoenix Picks New Jersey for Its First Foray in Eastern U.S." *Chronicle of Higher Education*, 23 October 1998

Selman, Gordon, and Paul Dampier. *The Foundations of Adult Education in Canada.* Toronto: Thompson Educational Publishers, 1991

Shorris, Earl. "On the Uses of a Liberal Education: As a Weapon in the Hands of the Restless Poor." *Harper's,* September 1997, 50–9

– *Riches for the Poor: The Clemente Course in the Humanities.* New York: W.W. Norton, 2000

Shumar, Wesley. *College for Sale: A Critique of the Commodification of Higher Education.* London: Falmer Press, 1997

Simon, Roger I., Don Dippo, and Arlene Schenke. *Learning Work: A Critical Pedagogy of Work Education.* New York: Bergen and Harvey, 1991

Slaughter, Sheila. "National Higher Education Policies in a Global Economy." In *Universities and Globalization: Critical Perspectives*, ed. Jan Currie and Janice Newson, 45–70. Thousand Oaks, Calif.: Sage Publications, 1998

Slaughter, Sheila, and Larry L. Leslie. *Academic Capitalism: Politics, Policies and the Entrepreneurial University*. Baltimore: Johns Hopkins University Press, 1997

Smith, David Geoffrey. "Economic Fundamentalism, Globalization and the Public Remains of Education." *Interchange* 30, no. 1 (1999): 93–117

Sokoloff, Heather. "Ontario May Get Private Universities." *National Post*, 31 July 2001

Sorger, George. McMaster University, cited in *Toronto Star*, 15 December 1997

Sorum, Christina Elliott. "'Vortex, Clouds and Tongue': New Problems in the Humanities?" *Daedalus* 128, no. 1 (1999): 241–64

"Special Feature on Higher Education." *Studio Two*. TVOntario, 4 September 2000

Stanford, Jim. "Why the Computer E-Emperor Has No Clothes." *Globe and Mail*, 23 March 2000

Stanton, Timothy K. "Liberal Arts, Experiential Learning and Public Service: Necessary Ingredients for Socially Responsible Undergraduate Education." *Journal of Cooperative Education* 27, no. 1 (1990): 55–68

Statistics Canada. "Adult Education and Training." *The Daily*. Summarized in <ocufalist@ocufa.on.ca> 18 June 1999

– "Average Hours Per Week of Television Viewing." <www.statcan.can/english/Pgdb/People/Culture/arts23.htm> Fall 1998

– "Part-Time University Faculty." *The Daily*. <www.statcan.ca:80/Daily/English/000830/d000830c.htm> 30 August 2000

– "University Degrees Granted by Field of Study, by Sex." <http:www.statcan.ca/english/Pgdb/People/Education/educ21.htm>

– "University Tuition Fees." *The Daily*.
<wysiwyg://12/http:www.statcan..c:8o/Daily/English/o1o827/do1o
827b.htm>27 August 2001

Stueck, Wendy. "Non-techies Stake Claim." *Globe and Mail,*
19 April 2000

*Teaching at an Internet Distance: The Pedagogy of Online Teaching
and Learning.* Report of a 1998–99 University of Illinois Faculty
Seminar. University of Illinois, 2000.
<www.vpaa.uillinois.edu/tid/report/tid_report.html>

"Technology Transfer to a New Level." *Chronicle of Higher Education,* 11 December 1998

Theobald, Steven. "Jobs, Output Drop: It's Scary Out There."
Toronto Star, 31 March 2001·

Toplak, Maggie, and Judith Wiener. "A Critical Analysis of Grade 3
Testing in Ontario." *Canadian Journal of Psychology* 16, no. 1
(2000): 65–85

Toronto Arts Council Web site <www.torontoartscouncil.org/> 2000

Toronto Board of Trade. *Beyond the Status Quo: A Business Perspective on Enhancing Post-secondary Education.* Toronto: Board
of Trade, February 1998

Towle, Angela, and Brian Jolly. "Case Studies: Recent Curriculum
Designs." In *Medical Education in the Millennium,* ed. Brian
Jolly and Lesley Rees, 42–53. New York: Oxford University
Press, 1998

Trow, Martin. "The Exceptionalism of American Higher Educa-
tion." In *University and Society: Essays on the Social Role of
Research and Higher Education,* ed. Martin Trow and Thorsten
Nybom, 156–72. London: Jessica Kingsley Publishers, 1991

Tuck, Simon, and Susan Bourette. "Nortel Cuts, Investors Run."
Globe and Mail, 16 February 2001

Tudiver, Neil. *Universities for Sale: Resisting Corporate Control
over Canadian Higher Education.* Toronto: James Lorimer, 1999

"University Research Libraries Continue to Slide in Rankings."
CUFA/BC wire. <http://www.cufa.bc.ca> 4 October 1999

Useem, Michael. "Corporate Restructuring and Liberal Learning."
   Liberal Education 81, no. 1 (1998): 18–23
– *Liberal Education and the Corporation: The Hiring and
   Advancement of College Graduates.* New York: Aldine de
   Gruyter, 1989
Valpy, Michael."Cuts to Culture Confirm Old Economic Thinking."
   Globe and Mail, 13 March 1999
Vanderleest, J. "The Purpose and Content of a Liberal Education."
   In *Liberal Education and the Small University in Canada*, ed.
   Christine Storm, 3–17. Montreal and Kingston: McGill-Queen's
   University Press, 1996
Veblen, Thorstein. *The Higher Learning in America: A Memoran-
   dum on the Conduct of Universities by Businessmen.* 1918;
   reprint, New York: A.M. Kelley, 1965
Wagner, Joseph. "A Subtle Tyranny: Rediscovering the Purpose of
   the Liberal Arts." *Interchange* 29 no. 3 (1998): 327–44
Warde, Ibrahim. "Conflicts of Interest on the Campus." *Le Monde
   Diplomatique*, March 2001
Wasylenki, Donald A., Carole A. Çohen, and Barbara R. McRobb.
   "Creating Community Agency Placements for Undergraduate
   Medical Education: A Program Description." *Canadian Medical
   Association Journal* 156, no. 3 (1997): 379–82
Weaver, Frederick Stirton. *Liberal Education: Critical Essays on
   Professions, Pedagogy and Structure.* New York: Teachers Col-
   lege, Columbia University, 1991
Whitaker, Reg, and Gary Marcuse. *Cold War Canada: The Making
   of a National Insecurity State.* Toronto: University of Toronto
   Press, 1994
White, Alvin M., ed. *Essays in Humanistic Mathematics.* Washing-
   ton: Mathematical Association of America, 1993
Whitehead, Alfred North. *The Aims of Education and Other
   Essays.* New York: Macmillan, 1929
Winston, Gordon C. "For-Profit Higher Education: Godzilla or
   Chicken Little." *Change* January/February 1999, 13–19

Woodward, Christel A. "Monitoring an Innovation in Medical Education: The McMaster Experience." In *Innovation in Medical Education: An Evaluation of Its Present Status*, ed. Zohair M. Nooman, Henk G. Schmidt, and Esmat S. Ezzat, 27–39. New York: Springer, 1990

Woody, Thomas. *A History of Women's Education in the United States*. 1929; reprint, New York: Octagon Books, 1966

Wright, Robert. *Hip and Trivial: Youth Culture, Book Publishing and the Greying of Canadian Nationalism*. Canadian Scholars Press, 2001

Index